Attempts to locate the original drawing of The Fire and Water Man by Caspar Neher have proved fruitless. This drawing is another version by Neher, and is reproduced by permission of the Caspar Neher Estate and the Theatre Collection of the Austrian National Library.

WORKS OF BERTOLT BRECHT

The Grove Press Edition
General Editor: Eric Bentley

Translators

Lee Baxandall

Eric Bentley

Martin Esslin

N. Goold-Verschoyle

H. R. Hays

Anselm Hollo

Christopher Isherwood

Frank Jones

Charles Laughton

Carl R. Mueller

Desmond I. Vesey

DIE HAUSPOSTILLE

Bertolt Brecht

MANUAL OF PIETY

A bilingual edition with English text by
Eric Bentley and Notes by Hugo Schmidt

GROVE PRESS, INC.

New York

A number of friends read some or all of the translated poems in manuscript. I should like to thank especially Randall Jarrell for marking passages that needed further work and Frank Jones who even offered alternative phrasings of his own—some of which have, with his permission, been absorbed into this text.

Those poems in the *Manual of Piety* that also occur in *Baal* were translated literally by Martin Esslin before I worked on them. They have already appeared in our published translation of *Baal,* and reappear here with Mr. Esslin's permission. (I have revised them to correspond to the revised German text as found in the *Manual.*) Mr. Esslin has also answered queries on a number of difficulties in other poems.

The debt of my collaborator, Hugo Schmidt, to Dr. H. O. Münsterer is acknowledged in the Notes. The debt to Dr. Münsterer's book on Brecht was increased by his willingness to write several letters in answer to questions. Dr. Schmidt also wishes to thank Dr. Pauline Jones for her advice on the French Symbolists.

Thanks are also owed to magazines that printed some of the poems in advance of book publication: *The New Republic, Act, The Tulane Drama Review, The Kenyon Review, Encounter.* One or two of the poems have appeared in books, specifically in *Varieties of Literary Experience,* ed. Stanley Burnshaw, New York University Press, 1962, and *The German Theatre Today,* ed. Leroy Shaw, University of Texas Press, 1963. On musical settings and recordings thereof, details are given in the Notes.

Thanks, finally, to Mr. Charles Rosenmeyer, a reader of mine who sent in an account of the music to "Memory of Marie A."

—E. B.

CONTENTS

American readers are getting to know their Brecht—backwards. They were given the late plays first, and now that they are being given the early plays, we often hear the query: Oh, did he begin as a poet? Bertolt Brecht did not exactly "begin as a poet"—he had completed a play by the time he was twenty—but he was a poet in his dramaturgy as well as in his lyrics. Epic theatre, as I have ventured to put it, is really lyric theatre. The epic theory can be represented by unfriendly critics as Brecht's attempt to make a virtue of the special limitation of his dramaturgy, the dramaturgy of a writer of ballads. To which one might retort that the epic form vindicated this dramaturgy and showed that indeed one *can* derive drama from poetic balladry. He who began by trying to excuse or conceal a limitation ended by transcending it. Conversely, when others who are not poets, or not poets of this kind, try to write Brechtian plays, they fail for at least two reasons: first, because they cannot achieve the quality of Brechtian songs, and second, because they cannot derive the rest of the drama from the songs, cannot write a drama that is poetic through and through. Prose dramatists who take up verse will never be Brechtian dramatists, because Brecht was a poet who took up drama or, rather, whose poetry spilled over into scenes and plays.

The time has come, then, to look at the poetry itself. *Manual of Piety* is one of the most remarkable books of first poems in modern literature; but by now that is the least of its claims on our attention. The word "first" only belittles it. Arguably, it is one of the best of all books of modern poems and certainly it is Bertolt Brecht's best book of poems. If it be retorted that this last claim rests on the fact that Brecht did not issue his later poems as books but piecemeal, the reply to this is that his *Svendborg Poems* were such a book and represents the Brecht of the thirties as amply as the *Manual of Piety* represents the Brecht of the twenties. More important, even when Brecht's collected poems are published, and it becomes manifest that many of his finest individual poems do not belong to the *Manual,* it will remain true that the *Manual* is the most impressive single group of poems that he wrote—impressive for the quality of individual items, for its singleness of vision and, within this unity, for range and variety of subject and statement.

This fact has not been more generally recognized because a literary Establishment existed that did not wish to recognize it. Or, doubling the problem, there were two Establishments that did not wish to recognize it. There was the Conservative Establishment, which would recognize among contemporary German poets only its own reactionary brother-in-arms, Gottfried Benn. (T. S. Eliot liked to quote Benn, but when I submitted *The Threepenny Opera* to Faber and Faber where, I understand, it was shown to Mr. Eliot, it was rejected.) And there was the Communist Establishment, which admired Bertolt Brecht for what he had in common with its own Johannes R. Becher, whose poetry will be forgotten any time the Communist government stops publishing it. In public, both Establishments have sought to kill *Manual of Piety* by ignoring it. I happen to have had the chance, however, to talk about the book with members of both Establishments, and they told me exactly the same thing: The book was an undergraduate spoof, a clever young man's gesture of rebellion calculated to *épater le bourgeois,* and nothing more. (Members of the Communist Establishment add that of course Brecht got on his feet later. And members of the Conservative Establishment would have said this had Brecht joined the Catholic Church.)

The element of "spoof," which is real enough in the book, is today not very interesting. If that was the only quality the book had ever possessed, it would by now have nothing. But frivolous spoofing is one thing, and serious parody is another: the latter is, I am inclined to think, the principal mode of the comic in our time. *Manual of Piety* is a sustained parody of a "manual of piety," that is, of "piety" and of "manuals" in their accepted forms. Sustained parody of the heroic is a familiar enough pattern in literature. Here we have—instead of the mock-heroic—the mock-pious, the mock-religious. The reason is surely not far to seek, particularly for those who will seek it in Brecht's own community, that of Germany. This is the country where modern cruelty has shown itself most loathsomely and most gigantically. It is also pre-eminently the country of pedantry and prissiness, propriety and punctilium. (Those who have not seen Germany itself have seen George Grosz's drawings.) Of this "correctness," "piety" is both the center and the symbol. That religion which is the opium of the people is also the incense of the bourgeoisie—a Tartuffian incense.

Jokes against religion will not have in 1965 the "shock value" they had in 1927, but this is only to repeat that *Manual of Piety* does not live on as a mere prank. What lives on is not a little dig at religion but a big point about it. One hears it said that Brecht's generation was the last to care about religion one way or the other, and that it is no longer possible to agonize as people did then over the question of whether God exists. If this were true, then a work like *Manual of Piety* would have lost more than its surface interest: it would have lost much of its very life. But is it true? Samuel Beckett and Ionesco belong to, and appeal to, a generation younger then Brecht's, and they are concerned almost wholly with the presence or absence of God. For the question of God merges with the question of meaning versus meaninglessness, the question of something versus nothing. It would be premature to assume that we have entered upon an era in which we can no longer say, with Emerson:

> And as the religious sentiment is the most real and earnest thing in nature, being a mere rapture, and excluding, when it appears, all other considerations, the vitiating this is the greatest lie. Therefore the oldest gibe of literature is the ridicule of false religion. This is the joke of jokes.

The ridicule of *false* religion? Is not Brecht attacking religion as such? Supernatural religion, yes. He proclaims that the skies are empty, that the universe is indifferent to man's fate. Yet like the Victorian atheists—with whom to such a large extent he belongs—he is unable to resist condemning that very God who does not exist. "Very slowly God forgot her bit by bit," he says of his "drowned girl." A mere manner of speaking? But for poets, manners of speaking are not "mere." A poem *is* a manner of speaking. And the phrase "God does not exist" can easily be a way of saying "God behaves as if he did not exist." Or, absence can be equated with nonexistence, as often it is by children.

A Catholic critic has applied to the early work of Brecht the phrase "the devil's prayer book," but he had the wisdom to put a question mark after it and, in his essay under that title, explained that, despite appearances, the *Manual of Piety* is not satanic but has a certain positive interest and value for Christians. The blasphemer is a man for whom the entities blasphemed against have great weight, and this antireligious *Manual of Piety* is full of the psychology we might call prereligious, meaning that it is found in persons who stand on the threshold of faith—vehement unbelief and outcry being (for some) a necessary preliminary. As for the content of Brecht's "antireligious" thought, is it, at this stage, any different from, say, Kierkegaard's assaults upon official Christianity?

"Ballad of Hannah Cash" ends with the exclamation, "May God make it up to her!" God stands accused, but on what grounds? Purely Christian ones. The sentiment at the base of the poem is the New Testament sympathy for the Magdalen and for the publicans and sinners generally. The metaphysical problem underlying the poem, then, is the problem of holding to the Christian sentiment when there is no Christian universe to support it. This is why the poem suggests an agony going far beyond its ostensible subject, which one can appreciate *a contrario* by reducing the poem to the bare narrative of Hannah Cash. To do so one would have to delete the references to indifferent nature (the weather, the geography), one would have to delete the last line, *and finally one would have to remove the poem from its context in the Manual of Piety*. The converse of this thought is that a book that may well have begun in Brecht's mind as a lark finally projects a vision utterly transcending the small images of the individual narrative ideas.

I do not see how this vision can reasonably be dismissed as narrow. Of course, if one wishes to play semantic games, one can define as narrow any view that differs from one's own: hence, to a game-playing Marxist or Catholic, *Manual of Piety* is narrow because it is not Marxist or Catholic. The word "narrowness" would have more serious application only if one could show that while Brecht dramatized one side of a situation, he overlooked the other. Applying this test, one will often find *Manual of Piety* less narrow than later Brecht works. For instance, on individualism. Brecht has been called the "anti-individualist." But that is the later Brecht. Here the anti-individualist appears in "Liturgy of the Breath" and "On the Self-Reliant." But "Ballad of the Secrets of Each and Every Man" deserves to be considered a classic statement of individualism: of the individualism that still remains possible after the old "self-reliance" has been seen through.

Nor can this double aspect of the vision be set aside as pointless broadmindedness, lack of point of view. It reflects, rather, an unusually successful attempt to grasp situations as a whole, to achieve an integral vision. Granted that the success is not achieved in a single massive poem, some modern *Divine Comedy,* it is achieved in a single *book* of poems. And that is a great deal. Enough, certainly, to justify presentation of this book as a whole by way of exhibiting Brecht's full stature as a poet.

The text itself will best demonstrate what kind of translations these are. Every kind of translation has its special liabilities. One can be a first-rate poet like Robert Lowell and write "imitations," which those who seek the other poet—the translated, not the translator—must find not imitative enough. One can be a first-rate linguist in two languages and produce a text whose literalness is guaranteed; yet this text may be no pleasure to read. And where is the poetry without the pleasure?

In pursuing a middle course between these extremes, I do not harbor the illusion that I have combined the best of both worlds. What I would hope is only that part of the pleasure taken in the process of translating is transmitted in the resulting translations. I began with the songs, that is, with those of the poems to which Brecht appended tunes. I made the German songs into English ones that could definitely be sung with pleasure and that might perhaps be heard with pleasure too. Then I applied myself to the other poems in the same spirit: I was writing for those who do not know the German and trying to bring them something of the experience that the German had brought to me.

I once collaborated with a translator who would translate a single adjective with three if he found three possible meanings lurking in it. This procedure can have a disastrous effect, since the length and shape of each speech are essential constituents of style. But if the translator instead opts for one of three such meanings, it would be good to let the reader know it. And, in the present volume, Hugo Schmidt does just this in his Notes, adding a great deal of other information not given in the translations themselves (or even sometimes in the original). What the translations lack in poetry can be supplied only by a poet, and at that a poet who miraculously happens to be Brecht reincarnated. What they lack in literal accuracy can in considerable measure be supplied in explanatory notes.

The German text is that of the 1927 edition, which differs in some points both from the privately printed *Taschenpostille* (Pocket Manual) of 1926 and from the *Manual of Piety* as reprinted in 1960 as part of the collected *Gedichte*. The one poem that appears in the 1926 *Taschenpostille* but not in the 1927 *Hauspostille* ("On His Mortality") is here reinstated.

It should perhaps be added that the division of labor between Hugo Schmidt and myself was not as sharp as the credits on the title page might suggest. I provided him with some of the material for his notes, and he provided me with amicably merciless criticisms of my translations.

—Eric Bentley

Berlin, Spring 1965

MANUAL OF PIETY

Die Hauspostille

DIE HAUSPOSTILLE

Inhaltsverzeichnis

MANUAL OF PIETY

Contents

DRITTE LEKTION: CHRONIKEN

VIERTE LEKTION: MAHAGONNYGESÄNGE

THIRD LESSON: CHRONICLES

FOURTH LESSON: MAHAGONNY SONGS

Diese Hauspostille ist für den Gebrauch der Leser bestimmt. Sie soll nicht sinnlos hineingefressen werden.

Die erste Lektion (Bittgänge) wendet sich direkt an das Gefühl des Lesers. Es empfiehlt sich, nicht zuviel davon auf einmal zu lesen. Auch sollten nur ganz gesunde Leute von dieser für die Gefühle bestimmten Lektion Gebrauch machen. Der in Kapitel 2 erwähnte Apfelböck, geboren zu München 1906, wurde 1919 durch einen von ihm an seinen Eltern begangenen Mord bekannt. Die in Kapitel 3 gezeichnete Marie Farrar, ein Jahr vorher wie der in Kapitel 2 erwähnte Apfelböck zu Augsburg am Lech geboren, kam vor Gericht wegen Kindesmordes in dem zarten Alter von 16 Jahren. Diese Farrar erregte das Gemüt des Gerichtshofes durch ihre Unschuld und menschliche Unempfindlichkeit. Der in Kapitel 9 erwähnte François Villon machte sich einen Namen durch einen Raubmordversuch und einige (wahrscheinlich obszöne) Gedichte.

Die zweite Lektion (Exerzitien = geistige Übungen) wendet sich mehr an den Verstand. Es ist vorteilhaft, ihre Lektüre langsam und wiederholt, niemals ohne Einfalt, vorzunehmen. Aus den darin verborgenen Sprüchen sowie unmittelbaren Hinweisen mag mancher Aufschluß über das Leben zu gewinnen sein. So betrachtet Kapitel 11 (Orges Antwort) gewisse Anfechtungen, die wenigen erspart bleiben, während Kapitel 5 (Historie vom verliebten Schwein Malchus) eine Warnung darstellt, durch Gefühlsüberschwang Ärgernis zu erregen.

Die dritte Lektion (Chroniken) durchblättere man in den Zeiten der rohen Naturgewalten. In den Zeiten der rohen Naturgewalten (Regengüsse, Schneefälle, Bankerotte usw.) halte man sich an die Abenteuer kühner Männer und Frauen in fremden Erdteilen; solche eben bieten die Chroniken, welche so einfach gehalten sind, daß sie auch für Volksschullesebücher in Betracht kommen. Bei einem Vortrag der Chroniken empfiehlt sich das Rauchen; zur Unterstützung der Stimme kann er mit einem Saiteninstrument akkordiert werden. Das Kapitel 2 (Ballade auf vielen Schiffen) ist zu lesen in Stunden der Gefahr: in ihm kommt der Gummimensch in Sicht. Die Männer vom Fort Donald in Kapitel 4 gehörten zu Eisenbahntrupps, welche quer durch die Wildnis der Rocky Mountains die ersten Schienen legten. Kapitel 6 (Ballade von den Seeräubern) ist hauptsächlich für die

This Manual of Piety is intended for the readers' use. It should not be senselessly wolfed down.

The First Lesson (Supplications) is directed straight at the readers' feelings. It is recommended that not too much of this lesson be read at any one time. Also, only quite healthy people should make use of this lesson, intended, as it is, for the feelings. The Apfelboeck who is mentioned in Chapter 2, born in Munich in 1906, became known in 1919 for a murder he perpetrated on his parents. The Marie Farrar specified in Chapter 3, born at Augsburg on the Lech one year before Apfelboeck, was tried for infanticide at the tender age of sixteen years. This Farrar touched the heart of the court by her guilelessness and human insensibility. The François Villon mentioned in Chapter 9 made a name for himself by an attempt at murder and robbery and several (probably obscene) poems.

The Second Lesson (Spiritual Exercises) is addressed more to the intellect. It is advantageous to read it slowly, repeatedly, never without simplicity of heart. From the sayings concealed therein, as also from the direct counsel, much information about life can be obtained. Thus, Chapter 11 (Orge's Answer) deals with certain temptations which few are spared, while Chapter 5 (Malchus, the Pig that Fell in Love) presents a warning against arousing scandal by excess of feeling.

The Third Lesson (Chronicles) should be leafed through at times when Nature is showing her naked powers. At times when Nature shows her naked powers (rainstorms, snowfalls, bankruptcies, etc.) one should find support in the adventures of brave men and women in foreign parts. The Chronicles include some such, which are put so simply they can even be considered for publication in grammar-school primers. At performances of the Chronicles smoking is recommended; to support the voice, the recital may be accompanied by a stringed instrument. Chapter 2 (Ballad Aboard Many Ships) is for reading during hours of danger; the India Rubber Man figures in it. The men of Fort Donald in Chapter 4 belonged to the railroad gangs which laid the first rails across the wilderness of the Rocky Mountains. Chapter 6 (Ballad of the Pirates) is chiefly intended for the bright nights of June; the second part of this ballad, insofar as its theme is a downfall (that of the pirates), can, however, be sung as late as October.

hellen Nächte im Juni bestimmt; der zweite Teil dieser Ballade, soweit er den Untergang behandelt, kann jedoch auch noch im Oktober gesungen werden. Die Melodie ist die von L'Etendard de la Pitié. Kapitel 8 (Von der Hanna Cash) gilt für die Zeit einer beispiellosen Verfolgung. (In der Zeit der beispiellosen Verfolgung wird die Anhänglichkeit eines Weibes offenbar werden.)

Die vierte Lektion (Mahagonnygesänge) ist das Richtige für die Stunden des Reichtums, das Bewußtsein des Fleisches und die Anmaßung. (Sie kommt also nur für sehr wenige Leser in Betracht.) Diese können die Gesänge ruhig mit der Höchstleistung an Stimme und Gefühl (jedoch ohne Mimik) anstimmen.

Es wird geben Tagzeiten des Andenkens und der frühen Geschehnisse. Die nachfolgenden fünf Kapitel der fünften Lektion (Die kleinen Tagzeiten der Abgestorbenen) sind für das Angedenken und die frühen Geschehnisse. Das zweite Kapitel von den verführten Mädchen ist zu singen unter Anschlag harter Mißlaute auf einem Saiteninstrument. Es hat als Motto: Zum Dank dafür, daß die Sonne sie bescheint, werfen die Dinge Schatten. Das dritte Kapitel vom ertrunkenen Mädchen ist mit geflüsterten Lippenlauten zu lesen. Das vierte Kapitel vom Liebestod ist gewidmet dem Andenken an das Liebespaar Franz Diekmann und Frieda Lang aus Augsburg. Das fünfte Kapitel vom toten Soldaten ist zum Gedächtnis des Infanteristen Christian Grumbeis, geboren den 11. April 1897 in Aichach, gestorben in der Karwoche 1918 in Karasin (Südrußland).

Nach der Lektüre der etwas düsteren Lektion von den kleinen Tagzeiten der Abgestorbenen sollte man das Schlußkapitel dazu lesen. Überhaupt empfiehlt es sich, jede Lektüre in der Taschenpostille mit dem Schlußkapitel zu beschließen.

Der Anhang (Vom armen B.B.) ist gewidmet George Pfanzelt, Caspar Neher und Otto Müllereisert, sämtliche aus Augsburg.

The tune is that of "L'Etendard de la pitié." Chapter 8 (Of Hannah Cash) is for a time of unprecedented persecution. (At a time of unprecedented persecution a woman's devotion will become manifest.)

The Fourth Lesson (Mahagonny Songs) is the right thing for hours of wealth, for fleshly awareness, for presumption. (Only, therefore, for very few readers is it relevant.) These are at liberty to strike up the songs with the greatest possible volume of voice and feeling (yet without gestures).

There will be appointed hours of remembrance and of past events. The following five chapters of the Fifth Lesson (The Little Hours of the Dead) are in memoriam and concern things past. Chapter 2, concerning the seduced girls, is to be sung while harsh dissonances are struck upon a stringed instrument. Its motto is: "Grateful that the sun shines on them, things cast shadows." Chapter 3, about the drowned girl, is to be read in a whisper. Chapter 4, about the love-death, is dedicated to the memory of the loving couple Franz Diekmann and Frieda Lang from Augsburg. Chapter 5, about the dead soldier, is in memory of Infantryman Christian Grumbeis, born April 11, 1897, in Aichach, died in Holy Week, 1918, in Karasin, Southern Russia.

After a reading of the somewhat somber lesson of the Little Hours of the Dead one should also read the final chapter. In general, it is recommended that every reading from the Manual of Piety be concluded with this final chapter.

The Appendix (On the Poor B.B.) is dedicated to George Pfanzelt, Caspar Neher, and Otto Muellereisert, all of them from Augsburg.

ERSTE LEKTION

Bittgänge

FIRST LESSON

Supplications

VOM BROT UND DEN KINDLEIN

1

Sie haben nicht gegessen
Das Brot im hölzernen Schrein
Sie riefen, sie wollten essen
Lieber die kalten Stein.

2

Es ist das Brot verschimmelt
Weil's keiner essen will.
Es blickte mild zum Himmel
Da sagte der Schrank ihm still:

3

„Die werden sich noch stürzen
Auf ein Stückelein Brot
Mit wenigen Gewürzen
Nur für des Leibes Not."

4

Es sind die Kindlein gangen
Viele Straßen weit.
Da mußten sie ja gelangen
Außer die Christenheit.

5

Und bei den Heiden da hungern
Kindlein dürr und blaß.
Es geben ihnen die Heiden
Keinem irgend was.

ON THE BREAD AND THE LITTLE CHILDREN

1

And they did not eat the
Bread in the oaken chest.
They yelled that they'd eat cold stones
Because cold stones are best.

2

And all the bread went moldy
That they would not eat.
While the bread looked mildly at the sky
The oak chest would repeat:

3

"They will live to throw themselves on
One little bit of bread
With very few spices in it
Just so they won't fall dead."

4

And walking many highways the
Children so far did come
They landed finally, as they must,
Outside Christendom.

5

And among the Heathen go hungry
Children all skin and bone.
And the Heathen don't give a single
Thing to anyone.

6

Sie würden sich gerne stürzen
Auf ein Stückelein Brot
Mit wenigen Gewürzen
Nur für des Leibes Not.

7

Das Brot aber ist verschimmelt
Gefressen von dem Vieh.
Woll's Gott, es hat einst der Himmel
Ein kleines Gewürzlein für sie.

6

So now they would throw themselves gladly
On one little bit of bread
With very few spices in it
Just so they won't fall dead.

7

But all the bread went moldy.
On it the cattle did feast.
Let's hope that Heaven will give them
One little spice at least!

APFELBÖCK
ODER
DIE LILIE AUF DEM FELDE

1

In mildem Lichte Jakob Apfelböck
Erschlug den Vater und die Mutter sein
Und schloß sie beide in den Wäscheschrank
Und blieb im Hause übrig, er allein.

2

Es schwammen Wolken unterm Himmel hin
Und um sein Haus ging mild der Sommerwind
Und in dem Hause saß er selber drin
Vor sieben Tagen war es noch ein Kind.

3

Die Tage gingen und die Nacht ging auch
Und nichts war anders außer mancherlei
Bei seinen Eltern Jakob Apfelböck
Wartete einfach, komme was es sei.

4

Und als die Leichen rochen aus dem Spind
Da kaufte Jakob eine Azalee
Und Jakob Apfelböck, das arme Kind
Schlief von dem Tag an auf dem Kanapee.

5

Es bringt die Milchfrau noch die Milch ins Haus
Gerahmte Buttermilch, süß, fett und kühl.

APFELBOECK

OR

THE LILY OF THE FIELD

1

And in the mild light Jacob Apfelboeck
Struck both his father and his mother down
And locked the bodies in the laundry chest
And went on living in the house alone.

2

The clouds, they swam along beneath the sky.
Around the house the summer winds were mild.
And Jacob Apfelboeck sat in the house.
Seven days before he had been still a child.

3

As days depart, and as the nights go by
Nothing is changed except a lot of things.
Home with his parents Jacob Apfelboeck
Just sits and waits for what tomorrow brings.

4

And when the bodies both began to smell
He went and purchased an azalea flower.
And Jacob Apfelboeck, unhappy child,
Slept on the sofa from that very hour.

5

The milk-woman brings the milk into the house
(A creamy buttermilk cool, sweet, and rich)

Was er nicht trinkt, das schüttet Jakob aus
Denn Jakob Apfelböck trinkt nicht mehr viel.

6
Es bringt der Zeitungsmann die Zeitung noch
Mit schwerem Tritt ins Haus beim Abendlicht
Und wirft sie scheppernd in das Kastenloch
Doch Jakob Apfelböck, der liest sie nicht.

7
Und als die Leichen rochen durch das Haus
Da weinte Jakob und ward krank davon.
Und Jakob Apfelböck zog weinend aus
Und schlief von nun an nur auf dem Balkon.

8
Es sprach der Zeitungsmann, der täglich kam:
Was riecht hier so? Ich rieche doch Gestank.
In mildem Licht sprach Jakob Apfelböck:
Es ist die Wäsche in dem Wäscheschrank.

9
Es sprach die Milchfrau einst, die täglich kam:
Was riecht hier so? Es riecht, als wenn man stirbt!
In mildem Licht sprach Jakob Apfelböck:
Es ist das Kalbfleisch, das im Schrank verdirbt.

10
Und als sie einstens in den Schrank ihm sahn
Stand Jakob Apfelböck in mildem Licht
Und als sie fragten, warum er's getan
Sprach Jakob Apfelböck: Ich weiß es nicht.

And what he does not drink goes down the drain
For Jacob Apfelboeck's not drinking much.

6

And in the evening comes the newspaper.
The man delivers it with heavy tread
And throws it with a bang into the box.
But Jacob Apfelboeck's not interested.

7

And as the smell of corpses filled the house
Young Jacob Apfelboeck fell sick and wept,
And, weeping, had to leave the sofa now.
Thenceforth upon the balcony he slept.

8

The man who brought the daily paper said:
What is that smell? It smells disgustingly.
In the mild light stood Jacob Apfelboeck.
The laundry in the laundry chest, said he.

9

And she who brought the daily milk exclaimed:
What is that smell? It smells like someone's dead.
In the mild light stood Jacob Apfelboeck.
The veal decaying in the cupboard, he said.

10

And when one day they looked into the chest
In the mild light stood Jacob Apfelboeck.
And when they asked him why he did the deed
I do not know, said Jacob Apfelboeck.

11

Die Milchfrau aber sprach am Tag danach
Ob wohl das Kind einmal, früh oder spät
Ob Jakob Apfelböck wohl einmal noch
Zum Grabe seiner armen Eltern geht?

11
But on the following day the milk-woman spoke:
That child, would he, at any hour of day,
Would Jacob Apfelboeck, would he ever go
To see the grave where his poor parents lay?

VON DER KINDESMÖRDERIN
MARIE FARRAR

1

Marie Farrar, geboren im April
Unmündig, merkmallos, rachitisch, Waise
Bislang angeblich unbescholten, will
Ein Kind ermordet haben in der Weise:
Sie sagt, sie habe schon im zweiten Monat
Bei einer Frau in einem Kellerhaus
Versucht, es abzutreiben mit zwei Spritzen
Angeblich schmerzhaft, doch ging's nicht heraus.
Doch ihr, ich bitte euch, wollt nicht in Zorn verfallen
Denn alle Kreatur braucht Hilf von allen.

2

Sie habe dennoch, sagt sie, gleich bezahlt
Was ausgemacht war, sich fortan geschnürt
Auch Sprit getrunken, Pfeffer drin vermahlt
Doch habe sie das nur stark abgeführt.
Ihr Leib sei zusehends geschwollen, habe
Auch stark geschmerzt, beim Tellerwaschen oft.
Sie selbst sei, sagt sie, damals noch gewachsen.
Sie habe zu Marie gebetet, viel erhofft.
Auch ihr, ich bitte euch, wollt nicht in Zorn verfallen
Denn alle Kreatur braucht Hilf von allen.

3

Doch die Gebete hätten, scheinbar, nichts genützt.
Es war auch viel verlangt. Als sie dann dicker war
Hab' ihr in Frühmetten geschwindelt. Oft hab' sie
geschwitzt
Auch Angstschweiß, häufig unter dem Altar.

ON THE INFANTICIDE
MARIE FARRAR

1

Marie Farrar, born in the month of April,
Rickets, no birthmarks, orphan, not of age,
Not previously in trouble, now maintains
She's killed an infant. This is how it happened.
When she was in her second month, she says,
She went to a woman living in a basement
And took two douches to abort the child,
Painful, she claims, although they didn't work.
But, sirs, I beg, do not give way to indignation.
Each creature needs the help of all creation.

2

And yet, she says, she paid the agreed amount
And henceforth laced herself up very tight
Drank kerosene with pepper ground into it:
Her bowels couldn't hold on to this, however.
Her body, swollen visibly, gave her
Much pain. She'd feel it when she washed the dishes.
She said she was still a growing girl at the time.
She prayed to the Virgin Mary, had high hopes.
And, sirs, I beg, do not give way to indignation.
Each creature needs the help of all creation.

3

And yet her prayers, it seems, had no effect.
It was a lot to ask. When she got bigger
She swooned at matins. And she often sweated
With anxious fear, not seldom at the altar.
Yet she contrived to keep her condition secret

Doch hab' den Zustand sie geheim gehalten
Bis die Geburt sie nachher überfiel.
Es sei gegangen, da wohl niemand glaubte
Daß sie, sehr reizlos, in Versuchung fiel.
Und ihr, ich bitte euch, wollt nicht in Zorn verfallen
Denn alle Kreatur braucht Hilf von allen.

4
An diesem Tag, sagt sie, in aller Früh
Ist ihr beim Stiegenwischen so, als krallten
Ihr Nägel in den Bauch. Es schüttelt sie.
Jedoch gelingt es ihr, den Schmerz geheimzuhalten.
Den ganzen Tag, es ist beim Wäschehängen
Zerbricht sie sich den Kopf; dann kommt sie drauf
Daß sie gebären sollte, und es wird ihr
Gleich schwer ums Herz. Erst spät geht sie hinauf.
Doch ihr, ich bitte euch, wollt nicht in Zorn verfallen
Denn alle Kreatur braucht Hilf von allen.

5
Man holte sie noch einmal, als sie lag:
Schnee war gefallen und sie mußte kehren.
Das ging bis elf. Es war ein langer Tag.
Erst in der Nacht konnte sie in Ruhe gebären.
Und sie gebar, so sagt sie, einen Sohn.
Der Sohn war ebenso wie andere Söhne.
Doch sie war nicht so wie die anderen, obschon:
Es liegt kein Grund vor, daß ich sie verhöhne.
Auch ihr, ich bitte euch, wollt nicht in Zorn verfallen
Denn alle Kreatur braucht Hilf von allen.

6
So will ich also weiter denn erzählen
Wie es mit diesem Sohn geworden ist

Until the time of the actual birth arrived.
For there was no one who believed that she,
So unattractive, gave way to temptation.
You, sirs, I beg, do not give way to indignation.
Each creature needs the help of all creation.

4

And on that day, she says, quite early on,
While washing stairs she felt that nails were clawing
Into her belly. And she gets the shivers.
Yet she succeeds in keeping this pain secret
And all day long while hanging out the washing
She racks her brains. And then it comes to her:
She's ready to give birth. Straightway her heart
Feels heavy. And she goes to bed quite late.
But, sirs, I beg, do not give way to indignation.
Each creature needs the help of all creation.

5

She lay in bed. They woke her up again.
For snow had fallen and she had to sweep it
Until eleven o'clock. A long, long day.
Only at night could she give birth in peace.
And she gave birth to a little son, she says.
Her son was very much like other sons
But she was not like other mothers, though
I have no reason to look down on her.
You, sirs, I beg, do not give way to indignation.
Each creature needs the help of all creation.

6

And so I shall continue with the story
About that son and what became of him

(Sie wollte davon, sagt sie, nichts verhehlen)
Damit man sieht, wie ich bin und du bist.
Sie sagt, sie sei, nur kurz im Bett, von Übel-
keit stark befallen worden und, allein
Hab' sie, nicht wissend, was geschehen sollte
Mit Mühe sich bezwungen, nicht zu schrein.
Und ihr, ich bitte euch, wollt nicht in Zorn verfallen
Denn alle Kreatur braucht Hilf von allen.

7

Mit letzter Kraft hab' sie, so sagt sie, dann
Da ihre Kammer auch eiskalt gewesen
Sich zum Abort geschleppt und dort auch (wann
Weiß sie nicht mehr) geborn ohn Federlesen
So gegen Morgen. Sie sei, sagt sie
Jetzt ganz verwirrt gewesen, habe dann
Halb schon erstarrt, das Kind kaum halten können
Weil es in den Gesindabort hereinschnein kann.
Auch ihr, ich bitte euch, wollt nicht in Zorn verfallen
Denn alle Kreatur braucht Hilf von allen.

8

Dann zwischen Kammer und Abort, vorher sagt sie
Sei noch gar nichts gewesen, fing das Kind
Zu schreien an, das hab' sie so verdrossen, sagt sie
Daß sie's mit beiden Fäusten ohne Aufhörn, blind
So lang geschlagen habe, bis es still war, sagt sie.
Hierauf hab' sie das Tote noch gradaus
Zu sich ins Bett genommen für den Rest der Nacht
Und es versteckt am Morgen in dem Wäschehaus.
Doch ihr, ich bitte euch, wollt nicht in Zorn verfallen
Denn alle Kreatur braucht Hilf vor allem.

(She wanted to hold nothing back, she says)
That all may see what you and I are like.
She was not long in bed, she says, when sickness
Came on her, sudden, strong. All she could think of
Was (not knowing what was going to happen)
To force herself by main strength not to scream.
And, Sirs, I beg, do not give way to indignation.
Each creature needs the help of all creation.

7

Then, with what strength remained, so she declares
(Her little room was also icy cold)
She crawled to the servants' privy. It was there
That she gave birth. No fuss. She can't say when
But toward morning. And she was now distracted,
Her fingers too benumbed to hold the child
For snow could get in through the privy roof.
You, sirs, I beg, do not give way to indignation.
Each creature needs the help of all creation.

8

Between the privy and her room—earlier, she says,
Nothing happened—the child began to cry
And this got on her nerves, she says, and then
She hit it with her fists unceasingly
And blindly till it quieted down, she says.
And thereupon she took the dead thing up
Into her bed for what remained of night.
When morning came she hid it in the washhouse.
But you, don't be indignant, for indeed
Help is what's needed most by all creation.

9

Marie Farrar, geboren im April
Gestorben im Gefängnishaus zu Meißen
Ledige Kindesmutter, abgeurteilt, will
Euch die Gebrechen aller Kreatur erweisen.
Ihr, die ihr gut gebärt in saubern Wochenbetten
Und nennt „gesegnet" euren schwangeren Schoß
Wollt nicht verdammen die verworfnen Schwachen
Denn ihre Sünd war schwer, doch ihr Leid groß.
Darum, ich bitte euch, wollt nicht in Zorn verfallen
Denn alle Kreatur braucht Hilf von allen.

9

Marie Farrar, born in the month of April,
Died: Meissen. In the penitentiary.
Unmarried mother. Found guilty. Demonstrating
The frailties of us creatures one and all.
You who give birth in snow-white childbed sheets
All you who call your pregnant bellies Blest
Do not condemn the outcast and the weak
For if their sin was grave, great was their grief.
Therefore, I beg, do not give way to indignation.
Each creature needs the help of all creation.

DAS SCHIFF

1

Durch die klaren Wasser schwimmend vieler Meere
Löst' ich schaukelnd mich von Ziel und Schwere
Mit den Haien ziehend unter rotem Mond.
Seit mein Holz fault und die Segel schlissen
Seit die Seile modern, die am Strand mich rissen
Ist entfernter mir und bleicher auch mein Horizont.

2

Und seit jener hinblich und mich diesen
Wassern die entfernten Himmel ließen
Fühl ich tief, daß ich vergehen soll.
Seit ich wußte, ohne mich zu wehren
Daß ich untergehen soll in diesen Meeren
Ließ ich mich den Wassern ohne Groll.

3

Und die Wasser kamen, und sie schwemmten
Viele Tiere in mich, und in fremden
Wänden freundeten sich Tier und Tier.
Einst fiel Himmel durch die morsche Decke
Und sie kannten sich in jeder Ecke
Und die Haie blieben gut in mir.

4

Und im vierten Monde schwammen Algen
In mein Holz und grünten in den Balken:
Mein Gesicht ward anders noch einmal.
Grün und wehend in den Eingeweiden

THE SHIP

Swimming through clear waters of many seas
Beneath red moons, beside the sharks, I freed
Myself from gravity and destination.
Since my wood rotted, since my sails all split,
And the ropes decayed that tied me to the pier
My horizon has been paler, more remote.
My horizon faded and the skies, remoter now,
Left me to my fate amid these waters
And something tells me I shall cease to be.
Knowing I'd not be able to run away
But one day would go under in these seas
I gave myself to the waters without complaint.
The waters fell upon me, and poured many
Beasts into me. Within these alien walls
Animal made friends with animal.
One day the sky fell through the rotten ceiling
And they all had each other in every corner.
The sharks held on inside me very firmly.
In the fourth month algae came swimming in-
to my wood; and they were green in the beams.
My face became quite different one last time.
Green, with a fluttering in my entrails, I
Sailed slowly on, no longer suffering much,
Heavy with moon and plant, with shark and whale.
I was a resting place for gulls and algae.
It is not my fault if I cannot save them.
When I go down, I shall be full and heavy.
Now, in the eighth month, the waters run into me
Much oftener. My face grows paler. I pray for the end.

Fishermen from far declared they saw
Something coming which dissolved while coming.

Fuhr ich langsam, ohne viel zu leiden
Schwer mit Mond und Pflanze, Hai und Wal.

5
Möv' und Algen war ich Ruhestätte
Schuldlos immer, daß ich sie nicht rette.
Wenn ich sinke, bin ich schwer und voll.
Jetzt, im achten Monde, rinnen Wasser
Häufiger in mich. Mein Gesicht wird blasser.
Und ich bitte, daß es enden soll.

6
Fremde Fischer sagten aus: sie sahen
Etwas nahen, das verschwamm beim Nahen.
Eine Insel? Ein verkommnes Floß?
Etwas fuhr, schimmernd von Mövenkoten
Voll von Alge, Wasser, Mond und Totem
Stumm und dick auf den erbleichten Himmel los.

Was it an island? A decrepit raft?
Something was moving, bright with seagull dung,
Full of algae, water, moon, dead objects,
Silent and broad toward the washed-out sky.

GESANG DES SOLDATEN DER ROTEN ARMEE

1

Weil unser Land zerfressen ist
Mit einer matten Sonne drin
Spie es uns aus in dunkle Straßen
Und frierende Chausseen hin.

2

Schneewasser wusch im Frühjahr die Armee
Sie ist des roten Sommers Kind!
Schon im Oktober fiel auf sie der Schnee
Ihr Herz zerfror im Januarwind.

3

In diesen Jahren fiel das Wort Freiheit
Aus Mündern, drinnen Eis zerbrach.
Und viele sah man mit Tigergebissen
Ziehend der roten, unmenschlichen Fahne nach.

4

Oft abends, wenn im Hafer rot
Der Mond schwamm, vor dem Schlaf am Gaul
Redeten sie von kommenden Zeiten
Bis sie einschliefen, denn der Marsch macht faul.

5

Im Regen und im dunklen Winde
War Schlaf uns schön auf hartem Stein.
Der Regen wusch die schmutzigen Augen
Von Schmutz und vielen Sünden rein.

HYMN OF THE RED ARMY SOLDIER*

1

Because beneath a leaden sun
This land of ours is gnawed away
It spat us out on freezing highways
It spat us out on byways dark.

2

Though washed in snow in time of spring
The army is red summer's child.
The fall brought snow. When it was winter
The army's heart froze in the wind.

3

In those years Freedom was a word
That often fell from lips of ice
And some had tigers' fangs that followed
After the red, inhuman flag.

4

When in the corn the red moon swam
Our fellows tied their horses up
And in the fields talked of the future,
Then fell asleep, tired by the march.

5

The rain it rained, the dark wind blew,
To sleep on stones was very sweet.
The rain removed from weary eyelids
Not just the dirt but many sins.

*Copyright © 1961 by *Encounter*.

6

Oft wurde nachts der Himmel rot
Sie hielten's für das Rot der Früh.
Dann war es Brand, doch auch das Frührot kam
Die Freiheit, Kinder, die kam nie.

7

Und drum: wo immer sie auch warn
Das ist die Hölle, sagten sie.
Die Zeit verging. Die letzte Hölle
War doch die allerletzte Hölle nie.

8

Sehr viele Höllen kamen noch.
Die Freiheit, Kinder, die kam nie.
Die Zeit vergeht. Doch kämen jetzt die Himmel
Die Himmel wären ohne sie.

9

Wenn unser Leib zerfressen ist
Mit einem matten Herzen drin
Speit die Armee einst unser Haut und Knochen
In kalte flache Löcher hin.

10

Und mit dem Leib, von Regen hart
Und mit dem Herz, versehrt von Eis
Und mit den blutbefleckten leeren Händen
So kommen wir grinsend in euer Paradeis.

6

And when at night the sky grew red
They took it for the red of dawn.
It was a fire. The dawn came later.
But Freedom never came, my boys!

7

And so wherever they might be
They said: this finally is hell.
But all the hells that once were final
Gave place to others finally.

8

So many hells were still to come.
But Freedom never came, my boys!
And now if what arrived were Heaven
They would not be around to see.

9

When we ourselves are gnawed away
(Our hearts as leaden as the sun)
The army spits our skin and bones out
Into a hole not deep but cold.

10

With bodies hardened by the rain
With hearts disfigured by the ice
With empty, bloody hands and grinning
We enter now your paradise.

LITURGIE VOM HAUCH

1

Einst kam ein altes Weib einher

2

Die hatte kein Brot zum Essen mehr

3

Das Brot, das fraß das Militär

4

Da fiel sie in die Goss', die war kalte

5

Da hatte sie keinen Hunger mehr.

6

Darauf schwiegen die Vöglein im Walde
Über allen Wipfeln ist Ruh
In allen Gipfeln spürest du
Kaum einen Hauch.

7

Da kam einmal ein Totenarzt einher

8

Der sagte: die Alte besteht auf ihrem Schein

LITURGY OF THE BREATH

1

Along came an old woman

2

She had no bread left to eat

3

The bread had all gone to the army

4

So she fell in the gutter, which was cold

5

And didn't go hungry any more.

6

At that the birds in the forest fell silent
On every treetop is rest
In every hilltop can be heard
Barely a breath.

7

Along came a doctor for an autopsy

8

He said the old girl wasn't shamming

9

Da grub man die hungrige Alte ein

10

So sagte das alte Weib nichts mehr

11

Nur der Arzt lachte noch über die Alte.

12

Auch die Vöglein schwiegen im Walde
Über allen Wipfeln ist Ruh
In allen Gipfeln spürest du
Kaum einen Hauch.

13

Da kam einmal ein einziger Mann einher

14

Der hatte für die Ordnung gar keinen Sinn

15

Der fand in der Sache einen Haken drin

16

Der war eine Art Freund für die Alte

17

Der sagte, ein Mensch müsse essen können, bitte sehr—

9

So they buried the hungry woman

10

And she didn't say anything more

11

But the doctor went on laughing about her.

12

And the birds in the forest fell silent too
On every treetop is rest
In every hilltop can be heard
Barely a breath.

13

Along came a man all by himself

14

A fellow with no respect for the established order

15

He figured there was a snag someplace

16

He felt kind of friendly to the old woman

17

He said: We all have to eat, don't we?

18

Darauf schwiegen die Vöglein im Walde
Über allen Wipfeln ist Ruh
In allen Gipfeln spürest du
Kaum einen Hauch.

19

Da kam mit einemmal ein Kommissar einher

20

Der hatte einen Gummiknüppel dabei

21

Und zerklopfte dem Mann seinen Hinterkopf zu Brei

22

Und da sagte auch dieser Mann nichts mehr

23

Doch der Kommissar sagte, daß es schallte:

24

So! jetzt schweigen die Vögelein im Walde
Über allen Wipfeln ist Ruh
In allen Gipfeln spürest du
Kaum einen Hauch.

25

Da kamen einmal drei bärtige Männer einher

18
At that the birds in the forest fell silent
On every treetop is rest
In every hilltop can be heard
Barely a breath.

19
Along came a commissioner all of a sudden

20
He had a rubber truncheon on him

21
And he beat the back of that man's head to pulp

22
Whereupon the man didn't say anything more

23
But the commissioner said (till the echoes rang):

24
That's that. The birds in the forest are silent now
On every treetop is rest
In every hilltop can be heard
Barely a breath.

25
Along, one day, came three bearded men

26
Die sagten, das sei nicht eines einzigen Mannes Sache allein.

27
Und sie sagten es so lang, bis es knallte

28
Aber dann krochen Maden durch ihr Fleisch in ihr Bein

29
Da sagten die bärtigen Männer nichts mehr

30
Darauf schwiegen die Vögelein im Walde
Über allen Wipfeln ist Ruh
In allen Gipfeln spürest du
Kaum einen Hauch.

31
Da kamen mit einemmal viele rote Männer einher

32
Die wollten einmal reden mit dem Militär

33
Doch das Militär redete mit dem Maschinengewehr

34
Und da sagten die roten Männer nichts mehr.

26
They said this was no situation for a man to handle by himself

27
And kept on saying it till the shooting started

28
But then maggots crawled through their flesh into their bones

29
And the bearded men didn't say anything more.

30
The birds in the forest fell silent
On every treetop is rest
In every hilltop can be heard
Barely a breath.

31
Along came many red men all of a sudden

32
They wanted to talk with the army

33
But the army talked with machine guns

34
And the red men didn't say anything more

35
Doch sie hatten auf ihrer Stirn noch eine Falte

36
Darauf schwiegen die Vögelein im Walde
Über allen Wipfeln ist Ruh
In allen Gipfeln spürest du
Kaum einen Hauch.

37
Da kam einmal ein großer roter Bär einher

38
Der wußte nichts von den Bräuchen hier, denn der
kam von überm Meer

39
Und der fraß die Vögelein im Walde

40
Da schwiegen die Vögelein nicht mehr
Über allen Wipfeln ist Unruh
In allen Gipfeln spürest du
Jetzt einen Hauch.

35
But they still had furrows on their brows.

36
At that the birds in the forest fell silent
On every treetop is rest
In every hilltop can be heard
Barely a breath.

37
Along, one day, came a big red bear

38
Who knew nothing of the local customs
because he came from overseas

39
And gobbled up the birds in the forest.

40
And the birds of the forest were silent no longer
On every treetop is unrest
In every hilltop can be heard,
This time, a breath.

PROTOTYP EINES BÖSEN

1

Frostzerbeult und blau wie Schiefer
Sitzend vor dem Beinerhaus
Schlief er. Und aus schwarzem Kiefer
Fiel ein kaltes Lachen aus.
Ach, er spie's wie Speichelbatzen
Auf das Tabernakel hin
Zwischen Fischkopf, toten Katzen:
Als noch kühl die Sonne schien.

2

Aber

3

Wohin geht er, wenn es nachtet
Der von Mutterzähren troff?
Der der Witwen Lamm geschlachtet
Und die Milch der Waisen soff?
Will er, noch im Bauch das Kälbchen
Vor den guten Hirten, wie?
Tief behängt mit Jungfernskälpchen
Vor die Liebe Frau Marie?

4

Ah, er kämmt sich das veralgte
Haar mit Fingern ins Gesicht?
Meint, man sieht so die verkalkte
Freche Schundvisage nicht?
Ach, wie macht er seine böse
Fresse zittern, arm und nackt?

PROTOTYPE OF A BAD MAN

1

Blue as slate, frostbite all over,
By the charnel house he slept.
As he sat there, from his black jaw
Laughter cold as icebergs crept.
And toward the House of God he
Spat that laughter out like drool
Twixt the fishheads and the dead cats
White the sun shone bright and cool.

2

But

3

In the night where can he go who
Drips with tears of mothers still?
Who hath drunk the milk of orphans,
Who the widow's lamb did kill?
With the young calf in his belly
Will he The Good Shepherd meet?
Girt with little scalps of virgins
Will he Lady Mary greet?

4

With his fingers, look, he combs his
Seaweed hair down on his brow.
Does he think one does not see his
Cheeky chunky kisser now?
Naked, poor, how he can tremble!
Note the palpitating snout!

Daß ihn Gott aus Mitleid löse
Oder weil ihn Schauder packt?

5

Sterbend hat er schnell gesch . . .
Noch auf seine Sterbestatt.
Aber wird er dort noch wissen
Was er hier gefressen hat?
Kalt hat man ihn mit dem Schlangen-
fraß des Lebens abgespeist.
Will man da von ihm verlangen,
Daß er sich erkenntlich weist?

Darum bitt' ich hiemit um Erbarmen
Mit den Schweinen und den Schweinetrögen!
Helft mir bitten, daß auch diese Armen
In den Himmel eingehn mögen.

So a pitying God will save him?
Or because he's chickened out?

5

As he died he took a quick crap
Right there on the bed of death.
Up in Heaven will he remember
What they fed him down on earth?
He was fobbed off rather coolly
With life's scraps and leftovers.
Is he now in duty bound to
Murmur: Thanks a lot, dear sirs?

Therefore Heaven's mercy now I pray
Both for the pigs and the troughs
    where they get their dinners
Pray with me that even suchlike sinners
Enter into Heaven's eternal day!

MORGENDLICHE REDE AN DEN BAUM GREEN

1

Ich habe Ihnen heute nacht bitter unrecht getan;
Ich konnte nicht schlafen, weil der Wind so laut war.
Als ich hinaus sah, bemerkte ich, daß Sie schwankten
Wie ein besoffener Affe. Ich schämte mich für Sie, Green.

2

Ich bekenne einfach, daß ich mich geirrt habe:
Sie haben den bittersten Kampf Ihres Lebens gekämpft.
Es interessierten sich Geier für Sie.
Sie wissen jetzt, was Sie wert sind, Green.

3

Heute glänzt die gelbe Sonne in Ihren nackten Ästen,
Aber Sie schütteln noch immer Zähren ab, Green?
Sie leben ziemlich allein, Green?
Ja, wir sind nicht für die Masse . . .

4

Ich konnte gut schlafen, nachdem ich Sie gesehen habe.
Aber Sie sind wohl müd' heute?
Entschuldigen Sie mein Geschwätz!
Es war wohl keine Kleinigkeit, so hoch heraufzukommen
zwischen den Häusern,
So hoch herauf, Green, daß der
Sturm so zu Ihnen kann, wie heute nacht?

EARLY MORNING ADDRESS TO A TREE CALLED "GREEN"*

1

I did you, Sir, a bitter wrong last night.
I could not sleep: so deafening was the wind.
When I looked out, I noticed you were swaying
Like a drunk monkey. I was ashamed for you, Green.

2

Let me simply confess I was mistaken:
You were fighting the bitterest battle of your life.
Vultures were getting interested in you.
Now you know your worth, Green.

3

Today the yellow sun is shining on your naked boughs
But you're still shaking the tears off, aren't you, Green?
You're rather alone, aren't you, Green?
Mass civilization isn't for us, is it?

4

I was able to get some sleep, Sir, after I'd seen you.
But you must feel tired today, no?
Forgive my idle chatter.
It was after all no small achievement to get up so high
Between the houses
Up so high that the storm can reach you,
Green, like last night?

VOM FRANÇOIS VILLON

1

François Villon war armer Leute Kind
Ihm schaukelte die Wiege kühler Föhn
Von seiner Jugend unter Schnee und Wind
War nur der freie Himmel drüber schön.
François Villon, den nie ein Bett bedeckte
Fand früh und leicht, daß kühler Wind ihm schmeckte.

2

Der Füße Bluten und des Steißes Beißen
Lehrt ihn, daß Steine spitzer sind als Felsen.
Er lernte früh den Stein auf andre schmeißen
Und sich auf andrer Leute Häuten wälzen.
Und wenn er sich nach seiner Decke streckte:
So fand er früh und leicht, daß ihm das Strecken schmeckte.

3

Er konnte nicht an Gottes Tischen zechen,
Und aus dem Himmel floß ihm niemals Segen.
Er mußte Menschen mit dem Messer stechen
Und seinen Hals in ihre Schlinge legen.
Drum lud er ein, daß man am Arsch ihm leckte
Wenn er beim Fressen war und es ihm schmeckte.

4

Ihm winkte nicht des Himmels süßer Lohn
Die Polizei brach früh der Seele Stolz
Und doch war dieser auch ein Gottessohn.—
Ist er durch Wind und Regen lang geflohn
Winkt ganz am End zum Lohn ein Marterholz.

FRIEND VILLON

1

François Villon: he was a poor man's son.
A cool breeze rocked the cradle of Villon.
And of his youth in wind and rain only
The open sky above was good to see.
Villon, who ne'er had bed, found out with ease
And early too he liked a nice cool breeze.

2

Bleeding of feet and chafing of the buttocks
Taught him small stones are sharper than great rocks.
Early he learned to cast the stone at men
Then to skin them and dance a jig on the skin.
And if he rolled with the punches, well he knew
That was exactly what he liked to do.

3

God's favor was not his. He was not able
To sit and gorge himself at God's high table.
In fellow creatures he must stick a blade
Then place his neck inside the noose they made.
Oh, kiss my ass! was his suggestion rude
If he was feeding and he liked the food.

4

He never looked for heavenly recompense
For the police had crushed his confidence.
Yet he too was a son of the Good Lord
And if he fled when the wet tempest roared
The gallows beckoned and was his reward.

5

François Villon starb auf der Flucht vorm Loch
Vor sie ihn fingen, schnell, im Strauch aus List—
Doch seine freche Seele lebt wohl noch
Lang wie dieses Liedlein, das unsterblich ist.
Als er die Viere streckte und verreckte
Da fand er spät und schwer, daß ihm dies Strecken schmeckte.

5

Fleeing arrest, Friend Villon cunningly
Died ere they caught him in the shrubbery.
But die that truant soul of his will never:
'Twill live on like this song of mine forever.
Late and with difficulty François found
He liked to stretch on all fours on the ground.

BERICHT VOM ZECK

1

Durch unsere Kinderträume
In dem milchweißen Bett
Spukte um Apfelbäume
Der Mann in Violett.

2

Liegend vor ihm im Staube
Sah man: da saß er. Träg.
Und streichelte seine Taube
Und sonnte sich am Weg.

3

Er schätzt die kleinste Gabe
Sauft Blut als wie ein Zeck.
Und daß man nur ihn habe
Nimmt er sonst alles weg.

4

Und gabst du für ihn deine
Und anderer Freude her;
Und liegst dann arm am Steine
Dann kennt er dich nicht mehr.

5

Er spuckt dir gern zum Spaße
Ins Antlitz rein und guckt
Daß er dich ja gleich fasse
Wenn deine Wimper zuckt.

REPORT ON THE TICK

1

In the milkwhite bed
Through our childhood dreams
The man in violet
Haunted the apple trees.

2

Lying in dust before him
One saw him sitting there:
Lazy. Stroking his dove.
Sunning himself on the path.

3

Treasures the smallest gift,
Sucks up blood like a tick.
So one will have just him
He takes all else away.

4

If you give up for him
Your joy and others' joy,
And after, sleep on stone,
He does not know you now.

5

Likes to spit in jest
In your face and glare
Seizing you the moment
When your eyelash flicks.

6

Am Abend steht er spähend
An deinem Fenster dort
Und merkt sich jedes Lächeln
Und geht beleidigt fort.

7

Und hast du eine Freude
Und lachst du noch so leis—
Er hat eine kleine Orgel
Drauf spielt er Trauerweis'.

8

Er taucht in Himmelsbläue
Wenn einer ihn verlacht
Und hat doch auch die Haie
Nach seinem Bild gemacht.

9

An keinem sitzt er lieber
Als einst am Totenbett.
Er spukt durchs letzte Fieber
Der Kerl in Violett.

6

Evenings he stands spying
At your window ledge
Noting your every smile
Going offended away.

7

If you have a joy
If you laugh ne'er so low,
He has a little organ
For playing funeral airs.

8

Leaps into blue heaven
If he's laughed to scorn
Yet he's made the shark in
The image of himself.

9

The bed he loves to sit at
Is a bed of death.
The man in violet
Haunts your final breath.

ZWEITE LEKTION

Exerzitien

SECOND LESSON

Spiritual Exercises

VOM MITMENSCH

1

Schon als ein Mann die Monde zählend
Ihn auszog wie an einem Stiel
Schrie er laut auf, als er rot, elend
Und klein aus einem Weibe fiel.
Sie warteten. Mit Schwamm und Leinen!
Sie grüßten mit Trompetenschall.
Sie wuschen mit gerührtem Weinen
Den Kot ihm ab. [Auf jeden Fall.]

2

Von nun an sind sie ihm gewogen.
Er ist ihr Kind, er ist ihr Mann.
Sie rühren, wenn er ausgezogen
Den Tünchnerkalk mit Tränen an.
Und wenn er frißt, so sind sie heiter
Sie fressen strahlend seinen Mist.
Er sieht: sie tragen schwarze Kleider
Wenn ihm sein Hund verendet ist.

3

Sie tun ihr Wort in seine Zähne.
Er sagt's. Sie haben's schon gesagt.
Es nagt das Bein an die Hyäne
Und die Hyän' ist angenagt.
Und nennt er seine Wolken Schwäne
So schimpfen sie ihn hungrig blind
Und zeigen ihm, daß seine Zähne
Genau wie ihre Zähne sind.

ON ONE'S FELLOW MAN

1

When, counting months, a man had pulled him
Out on a stalk he gave a yell
As tiny, red, and miserable
Out of a woman's womb he fell.
They are waiting there. With sponge and linen!
To welcome him their trumpets play.
They wash the dirt from off his body
With heartfelt tears. Why shouldn't they?

2

Henceforth they show him their affection.
He is their child. He is their man.
They paint his room when he vacates it
And shed tears in the whitewash can.
And when he feeds, Oh, they are merry!
Beaming, they munch his excrement.
He sees that they are wearing black if
His dog perchance has met his end.

3

Their words between his teeth inserted
He says what they have said before.
(Hyenas gnaw at leg and torso:
They were themselves gnawed at of yore.)
And if he says his clouds are swans, then
They give it to him strong and hot
And show him that the teeth he's got are
Exactly like the teeth *they've* got.

4

Sie setzen sich in seine Träume
[Da, wo er wohnt, sind ihre Räume.]
Sie schlachten ihm ihre letzte Kuh
[Und schauen ihm beim Essen zu.]
Versalzen's mit gerührten Tränen
Und gehen, wenn er's ißt, nicht fort.
Sie zählen grinsend seine Zähne
Und warten gläubig vorm Abort.

5

Und um ihm menschlich nahzukommen,
Drehen sie ihm ihre Schwester an
Und netzen sie mit Bibelsprüchen
So daß er sie besteigen kann.
Und ihm lächelnd das Glück anfeuchtend
Wünschen sie angenehme Ruh.
Und ihn mit Scheinwerfern beleuchtend
Hören sie ihm durch Drähte zu.

6

Denn sie sind keine Ungeheuer
Und er ist nicht der gute Hirt
Sie legen die Hand für ihn ins Feuer
Und weinen, wenn er schwächer wird.
Dann zeigen sie ihm rote Bälge
Und sagen, wenn er sie vertrieb:
Das Ding, das die Geliebte melke
Das sei die Frucht, die von ihm blieb.

7

Er lebt in Furcht vor ihrem Grauen
Wenn sein Gefühl ihn überschwemmt.

4

Their dwellings also are his dwellings
And they invade his every dream.
For his sake their last cow they slaughter
And while he eats it look at him.
And with their tears they oversalt it
And while he eats they all stay on.
Grinning, they count his teeth, and loyal
They wait for him outside the john.

5

They palm their sister off upon him
To demonstrate how kind they are
Bless her with sayings from the Bible
To help him get on top of her.
Smiling, they lubricate his plaything
And wish him very pleasant nights
Listen to him with wired gadgets
And light him up with their searchlights.

6

For after all they are not monsters
And is he the Good Shepherd? No.
They stick their hands in the fire for him.
Should he grow weak, their tears flow.
Red brats they show to him, affirming,
When he has tried to banish them
The thing that's milking his beloved
Is all that now remains of him.

7

He lives in fear of their horror
Should feeling dominate his mind.

Denn nahmen ihm die Haut die Schlauen
So ließen sie ihm doch das Hemd.
Er trug den Leib in manchem Hemde
Verstohlen durch das Tageslicht.
Er starb. Und die Geliebte kämmte
Ihm schnell die Haare ins Gesicht.

8

Sie hat an seinem Leib gelegen
Sie hat ihn satt der Welt gemacht
Sie sah sich seine Lider regen
Sie hat sein Schlafen überwacht.
Sie hat ihm ihre Sklavenkette
Tief in sein mildes Fleisch gewetzt
Er hat ihr auf dem Totenbette
Sein letztes Wort noch übersetzt.

For though they flayed his skin they slyly
Made sure to leave his shirt behind.
In many a shirt he bore his body
In light, by stealth, from place to place.
And then he died. And his belovèd
Combed his hair down onto his face.

8

She's lain beside him, and she's caused him
To find life in this world too hard.
She's noted when his eyelid flickers.
When he is sleeping, she's kept guard.
Sorely she chafed his tender flesh with
The chain of their cohabitation.
He then upon his deathbed uttered
His last words to her—in translation.

ORGES GESANG

Orge sagte mir:

1
Der liebste Ort, den er auf Erden hab'
Sei nicht die Rasenbank am Elterngrab.

2
Orge sagte mir: Der liebste Ort
Auf Erden war ihm immer der Abort.

3
Dies sei ein Ort, wo man zufrieden ist
Daß drüber Sterne sind und drunter Mist.

4
Ein Ort sei einfach wundervoll, wo man
Wenn man erwachsen ist, allein sein kann.

5
Ein Ort der Demut, dort erkennst du scharf
Daß du ein Mensch nur bist, der nichts behalten darf.

6
Ein Ort, wo man, indem man leiblich ruht
Sanft, doch mit Nachdruck, etwas für sich tut.

HYMN OF ORGE*

Orge said to me:

1

The dearest place on earth was not (he'd say)
The grassy plot where his dead parents lay;

2

Said Orge: Of the places I recall
The privy is the dearest of them all.

3

It is a place where we rejoice to know
That there are stars above and dung below;

4

A place, once we are old enough, where we
Can get away—O joy!—from company;

5

A place that teaches you (so Orge sings):
Be humble, for you can't hold on to things;

6

A place where one can rest and yet where one
Gently but firmly can get business done;

---

*Copyright © 1962 by Eric Bentley and Martin Esslin.

7
Ein Ort der Weisheit, wo du deinen Wanst
Für neue Lüste präparieren kannst.

8
Und doch erkennst du dorten, was du bist:
Ein Bursche, der auf dem Aborte—frißt!

7

A place of wisdom where one has the leisure
To get one's paunch prepared for future pleasure.

8

And yet you learn there what you are (he said):
A chap who on a privy seat gets fed.

ÜBER DEN SCHNAPSGENUSS

1

In dem grünen Kuddelmuddel
Sitzt ein Aas mit einer Buddel
Grünem Schnaps. [Grünem Schnaps.]
Sitzt ein Aas mit einer Buddel
Und Herzklaps.
[Und Herzklaps.]

2

Sehet an, Josef, den Keuschen,
Zwischen ungeheuren Fleischen
Sitzt und schnullt. Sitzt und schnullt
An den Fingern, an den keuschen, aus Unschuld.
[Aus Unschuld.]

3

Sieben Sterne schmecken bitter.
Süß gezupfte Magenzitter
Macht sie gut. Macht sie gut.
Sieben Lieder, sieben Liter, das gibt Mut.
[Das gibt Mut.]

4

Linsel Klopps ging grad wie'n Meier.
Doch nun ist ihm auch viel freier
Seit er schwankt. Seit er schwankt.
Ach du Schwan in seinem Weiher, sei bedankt.
[Sei bedankt!]

ABOUT THE ENJOYMENT OF GIN

1

Down in pea-green fuddle-muddle
Sits a carcass with a boodle-bottle
Of pea-green gin. (Of pea-green gin.)
Sit a carcass with a boodle-bottle
And a weak heart within.
(Weak heart within.)

2

Look at Joseph, chaste little Joey!
Twixt female hills of fleshy snow, he
Doth sit and suck! (Sit and suck!)
Sucks his fingers, chaste little fingers, oh, the
Innocent schmuck!
(Innocent schmuck!)

3

"Seven Star" is rather bitter.
Pluck the guts of your twitter-zither
To make it sweet. (Make it sweet.)
Seven Lieder, seven Liter,
Put you on your feet.
(You on your feet.)

4

Linsel Klopps walked most sedately
But he learned to stagger lately
And he feels much freer. (Feels much freer.)
In this man's pond thou swan so stately
Accept a cheer!
(Accept a cheer!)

VORBILDLICHE BEKEHRUNG
EINES BRANNTWEINHÄNDLERS

1

Hinter Gläsern, an dem Schanktisch mit den
Schweren Lidern, Lippen violett
Trüben Augen in dem schweißigen Antlitz
Sitzt ein Branntweinhändler bleich und fett.
Seine schmierigen Finger zählen
Geld in einen Sack hinein:
In des Branntweins ölige Lache
Sinkt sein Kopf, und er schläft ein.

2

Und sein schwerer Leib, er wälzt sich ächzend
Kalter Schweiß klebt auf der Stirn wie Schleim
Und in seinem schwammigen Gehirne
Sucht ein schrecklich böser Traum ihn heim.
Und er träumt: er ist im Himmel
Und er muß vor Gottes Thron
Und trinkt Schnaps vor Angst und ist nun
Bis zum Halse voll davon.

3

Sieben Engel halten ihn umringet
Und er schwankt in seinen beiden Knien
Doch sie führen ihn, den Branntweinhändler
Stumm vor Gottes weißen Thron nun hin.
Seine schweren Lider heben
Kann er nicht in Gottes Licht
Und er fühlt die Zunge kleben
Blau, mit scheußlichem Gewicht.

EXEMPLARY CONVERSION
OF A BRANDY PEDDLER

1

At his bar, behind his glasses, with his
Heavy eyelids, lips of violet,
Bleary eyes set in a sweaty visage,
Sits a brandy peddler pale and fat.
And he counts out cash in his cashbox
With his hands which are wet with ooze.
In an oily pool of brandy
Falls his head as he takes a snooze.

2

And his heavy form rolls over, groaning,
And sweat rises from his brow like steam.
To his spongy cerebrum to haunt him
Comes a sinister and frightful dream.
And he dreams he is up in heaven
And to God's throne must now draw near
And in fear he drinks his brandy
Till he's full right up to here.

3

Seven angels make a ring around him
And he feels his legs are not his own.
But they lead the speechless brandy peddler
Right before Jehovah's gleaming throne.
And he cannot raise his eyelids
To the light of the Holy One
For his tongue is blue and sticky
And it weighs about a ton.

4

Und er sieht sich um nach einer Hilfe
Und er sieht in grünem Algenlicht:
Vierzehn Waisenkindlein schwimmen weinend
Flußab mit vergehendem Gesicht.
Und er sagt: es sind nur sieben
Weil ich so besoffen bin.
Doch er sagt es nicht: die Zunge
Will nicht an die Zähne hin.

5

Und er sieht sich um nach einer Hilfe
Bei den Männern, die er karten sieht
Und er schreit: Ich bin der Branntweinhändler!
Doch sie schreien ihr besoffen Lied.
Und sie schreien sich um ihre
Seligkeit voll Schnaps und blind.
Und er sieht an grünen Flecken
Daß sie fast verfault schon sind.

6

Und er sieht sich um nach einer Hilfe
Und er sieht: er steht im Hemd am Thron!
Steht im Hemd im Himmel, hört sie fragen:
Hast du all dein Kleid versoffen schon?
Und er sagt: Ich hatte Kleider
Und sie sagen: Keine Scham?
Und er weiß: Hier standen viele,
Denen ich die ihren nahm.

7

Und er sieht sich nicht mehr um nach Hilfe
Und er fällt aufs Knie hin, daß es klatscht

4

When he looks around in hope of succor
He beholds, all in the swamp-green light,
Fourteen orphan kids in tears and swimming
Down the stream and almost out of sight.
And he says: there are only seven
For I've drunk such an awful lot.
But he does not really say it
Since his tongue sticks in his throat.

5

When he looks around in hope of succor
At the gamblers whom he sees at play
Loud he shouts: I am the brandy peddler!
But they only shout their drunken lay.
And they shout away their salvation
For they're up to the ears in drink.
And his eyes tell him they're rotting
And his nose tells him they stink.

6

When he looks around in hope of succor
Something tells him and straightway he knows
He's in heaven with nothing but his shirt on
And they're asking: Peddler, where's your clothes?
And he says: But I did have clothes on!
You should be ashamed, they say.
And he knows that here are many
All whose clothes he took away.

7

And it's too late now to look for succor.
He falls to his knees with quite a smack.

Und er fühlt das Schwert im Fleisch am Nacken
Und das Hemd, das naß von Schweiß dran patscht:
Und er schämt sich vor dem Himmel
Und er fühlt im Innern drin:
Gott hat mich verstoßen jetzt, weil
Ich ein Branntweinhändler bin.

8

Und erwacht: mit schweren Lidern, stieren
Augen und den Lippen violett.
Doch er sagt zu sich: Nie wieder je bin
Ich ein Branntweinhändler, bleich und fett.
Sondern nur für Waisenkinder
Säufer, Greis und Dulderin
Gebe ich in Zukunft dieses
Segenlose Schmutzgeld hin.

And he feels a sword between his shoulders,
Wringing wet the shirt upon his back.
And he tells the Good Lord he's sorry
And he hears a small voice within:
God has banished you from his heaven
'Cause selling brandy is a sin.

8

And he wakes: with staring eyes and heavy
Eyelids and those lips of violet.
After this (he tells himself) he'll never
Be a brandy peddler pale and fat.
And you'll have to be an orphan
Drunkard, bum, or sufferer
If you want the filthy lucre
That's in my cash register!

HISTORIE VOM
VERLIEBTEN SCHWEIN MALCHUS

1

Hört die Mär vom guten Schwein
Und von seiner Liebe!
Ach es wollt geliebet sein
Und bekam nur Hiebe.

2

Weil's dem Schwein noch nie so war
[Erste, grüne Liebe!]
Liebte es mit Haut und Haar.
Und bekam nur Hiebe.

3

Denn die Sonne selber war
Diese große Liebe.
Wie, wenn sie's mit Haut und Haar
Zur Verzweiflung triebe?

4

Einmal nun im Sonnenschein
Kriegt es keine Hiebe
Und es schrie das gute Schwein:
Ist das nun nicht Liebe!?

5

Und das sehr beglückte Schwein
Es beschloß zu handeln
Um im ewigen Sonnenschein
Nun hinfort zu wandeln.

MALCHUS,
THE PIG THAT FELL IN LOVE

1

Worthy Malchus fell in love.
You will hear how this pig
Wanted to be loved in turn
And only took a beating.

2

First green love! He'd never dreamt
There were such sensations!
He felt good from snout to tail
But only took a beating.

3

For it was the sun herself
Who'd aroused this passion
And this pig from snout to tail
Drove to desperation.

4

One day in the sunshine bright
He *didn't* take a beating.
So that's love, I see, I see!
Was his exclamation.

5

And the much encouraged pig
Planned some further action:
In everlasting sunshine he'd
Do a little walking.

6

Und indem es Schweine fing
Daß sie sich verbeugten
Wenn das Schwein vorüberging
Ehrfurcht ihm bezeugten

7

Hoffte das begabte Schwein
Ihr zu imponieren
Und im guten Sonnenschein
Ständig zu spazieren.

8

Doch die Sonne sieht wohl nicht
Jedes Schwein auf Erden
Und sie wandt ihr Augenlicht
Ließ es dunkel werden.

9

Dunkel um das arme Schwein
Außen und auch innen.
Doch da fiel ihm etwas ein
Um sie zu gewinnen.

10

Und mit einem anderen Schwein
Übte es zusammen
Mit dem Rüssel Gift zu spein
Mit den Augen Flammen.

6

And since he forced some pigs to
Make a pretty curtsy
When it chanced our pig passed by
They bowed low before him.

7

So our pig expects to make
An impression on her
And forever walk around
In the golden sunshine.

8

But the great sun does not see
Every little porker
And she turned away her light
Leaving all in darkness.

9

And the dark attacked our pig
Outside and inside him.
But he had a brainstorm. He
Had figured how he'd win her.

10

And he practiced several tricks
(Another porker helped him):
Spitting poison with his snout,
Fire from his eyeballs!

11

Und ein altes schwarzes Schwein
Zwang es [nur durch Reden]
Ihm und seinen Schweinerein
Algier abzutreten.

12

Und als nun die Sonne kam
Tat es voll Erregung
Halberstickt von edler Scham
Eine Fußbewegung

13

In der alles lag, was je-
mals ein Schwein empfunden
(Liebe läßt vergessen Weh
Und gesalzene Wunden!)

14

Und so legt nun diese Sau
Auf 'ner kleinen Wiesen
Tieferschüttert seiner Frau
Afrika zu Füßen.

15

Und diktiert zur selben Stund'
Daß es einfach alle
Die ihm diesen Seelenbund
Störten, niederknalle.

11

He compelled one black old pig
Just by talking to him
To surrender Algiers to
Him and his swinish doings.

12

Overcome with noble shame
Awesomely exalted
When the sun rose Malchus moved
Four feet in obeisance.

13

In that movement of the feet
Was so much pure feeling!
(You can put salt in Love's wounds:
Love will overlook it!)

14

So this pig, moved to the soul,
In a little meadow
Lays all Africa at the
Feet of his fair lady.

15

At the same time he decrees
He will take those who would
Thwart this sacred bond of his
And grind them all to powder.

16

Und an dunklen Tagen, wenn
Sie ihm brach die Treue
Lief es finster weg vom Trog
Watschelte ins Freie.

17

Und man sah dort, wie das Vieh
Das erschreckend blaß war
Wütend in die Wolken spie
Bis es selber naß war.

18

Ja, in einer trüben Früh
In der Brunnenkresse
Drohte es ihr, daß es sie
Einstmals doch noch fresse.

19

Da sie alles fressen, mein-
te es dies wohl ehrlich;
Aber wo die Sonne scheint
Fressen Schweine schwerlich.

20

Aber jedes Schwein ist schlau
Weiß, die Sonn' im Himmelsblau
Ist stets nur die liebe Frau
Von der jeweils größten Sau.

16

And on gloomy days when she
Was unfaithful to him
He ran darkly from the trough
Shambling in the open.

17

And one saw the worthy swine
Grow a great deal paler.
Fuming, he spat at the clouds
And got wet all over.

18

And, one melancholy dawn,
Midst the water cresses,
He averred that one day he'd
Make a supper of her!

19

As pigs gobble all things, no
Doubt he must have meant it.
Yet the sun up in the sky's
Rather hard to get at.

20

Pigs aren't stupid, though. They see,
Though the sun's in heaven, she
Remains the well-loved wife of the
Great pig of this century.

VON DER FREUNDLICHKEIT DER WELT

1

Auf die Erde voller kaltem Wind
Kamt ihr alle als ein nacktes Kind
Frierend lagt ihr ohne alle Hab
Als ein Weib euch eine Windel gab.

2

Keiner schrie euch, ihr wart nicht begehrt
Und man holte euch nicht im Gefährt.
Hier auf Erden wart ihr unbekannt
Als ein Mann euch einst nahm an der Hand.

3

Und die Welt, die ist euch gar nichts schuld:
Keiner hält euch, wenn ihr gehen wollt.
Vielen, Kinder, wart ihr vielleicht gleich.
Viele aber weinten über euch.

4

Von der Erde voller kaltem Wind
Geht ihr all bedeckt mit Schorf und Grind.
Fast ein jeder hat die Welt geliebt
Wenn man ihm zwei Hände Erde gibt.

ON THE WORLD'S KINDNESS*

1

To this earth whereon the winds are wild
Each of you came as a naked child.
Owning nothing, your body froze
Till a woman gave you swaddling clothes.

2

No one called you. You were not besought.
In no handsome carriage were you brought.
On this earth you were unknown
When a man took your hand in his own.

3

And the world, it is not in your debt.
No one stops you if you try to quit.
Many never gave you a thought, my dears!
Many, though, on your account shed tears.

4

From this earth whereon the winds are wild
You depart with scurf and scab defiled.
Almost all have called the world their friend
Before they get their handful of earth in the end.

---

*Copyright © 1956 by *The New Republic*.

BALLADE VON DEN SELBSTHELFERN

1

Noch sitzen sie rauchend da
Im grünen Strandgesträuch
Da wird schon ihr Himmel
Verkümmert und bleich.

2

Sie haben mit Branntwein wohl
Ihr Herze kühn gemacht?
Da sehen sie staunend
Die Schwärze der Nacht.

3

Sie trinken? Sie lachen noch?
Gelächter steigt wie Rauch
Und plötzlich, verrückt, hängt
Der Mond rot im Strauch.

4

Ihr Himmel verbleicht wohl schon?
Wie schnell es doch geschah!
Ihr Tag ist schon nicht mehr
Und sie sind noch da?

5

Sie wiehern wohl immer noch?
„Selbst hilft sich der Mann?"
Da weht sie ein Hauch an
Vom morschenden Tann:

ON THE SELF-RELIANT

1

And smoking they sit in
Green shrubs on the beach.
The sky is beginning to
Turn wasted and pale.

2

Have they managed to get up
Their courage with schnapps?
Astounded they notice
The blackness of night.

3

Are they drinking? And laughing?
Horselaughs rise like smoke.
Weirdly, all at once, the
Red moon's in the trees.

4

Their sky's turning pale, hm?
And how fast this occurred!
They've all had their day yet
Are they still around?

5

Still horselaughing, are they?
"No help like self-help!"
And a breath whispers to them
From the rotting woods:

6
Die trostlosen Winde wehn
Die Welt hat sie satt!
Und schweigend verläßt sie
Der Abend im Watt.

6

The comfortless winds blow.
The world's sick of them.
The silent night leaves them
Out on the mud flats.

ÜBER DIE ANSTRENGUNG

1

Man raucht. Man befleckt sich. Man trinkt sich hinüber
Man schläft. Man grinst in ein nacktes Gesicht.
Der Zahn der Zeit nagt zu langsam, mein Lieber!
Man raucht. Man geht k . . . Man macht ein Gedicht.

2

Unkeuschheit und Armut sind unsere Gelübde
Unkeuschheit hat oft unsere Unschuld versüßt.
Was einer in Gottes Sonne verübte
Das ist's, was in Gottes Erde er büßt.

3

Der Geist hat verhurt die Fleischeswonne
Seit er die haarigen Hände entklaut
Es durchdringen die Sensationen der Sonne
Nicht mehr die pergamentene Haut.

4

Ihr grünen Eilande der tropischen Zonen
Wie seht ihr aus morgens und abgeschminkt!
Die weiße Hölle der Visionen
Ist ein Bretterverschlag, worin Regen eindringt.

5

Wie sollen wir uns, die Bräute, betören?
Mit Zobelfleischen? ah, besser mit Gin!
Einem Lilagemisch von scharfen Likören
Mit bittren ersoffenen Fliegen darin.

ON EXERTION

1

One smokes, one defiles oneself, drinks oneself silly,
One sleeps and one grins into some naked face.
For Father Time's tooth gnaws too slowly, old fellow!
One smokes and one shits and one makes up some verse.

2

Unchastity often our innocence sweetened
(Unchastity, poverty: these are our vows).
What a man has practiced in God's sunshine
Is what he atones for in God's good earth.

3

The brain's made a whore of delight in the body
Into rude hairy fingers untwisting our claws.
Sensations of sunshine can't penetrate parchment
Or skin that, like parchment, is callous and hard.

4

O all you green islands of tropical regions
How you look in the morning without your make-up!
For the pallid inferno of all human visions
Is a shack of thin boards with the rain leaking through.

5

How shall we bewitch our brides—and ourselves, too?
With meat of the sable? No, better with gin
And with piquant liqueurs of a lilac color
With drowned and bitter flies in them!

6

Man säuft sich hinauf bis zum Riechgewässer.
Die Schnäpse verteilt man mit schwarzem Kaffee.
Dies alles verfängt nicht, Maria, 's ist besser
Wir gerben die köstlichen Häute mit Schnee!

7

Mit zynischer Anmut leichter Gedichte
Einer Bitternis mit Orangegeschmack
In Eis gekühlt! malaiisch gepichte
Haare im Auge! oh, Opiumtabak

8

In windtollen Hütten aus Nankingpapier
O du Bitternisfrohsinn der Welt
Wenn der Mond, dieses sanfte, weiße Getier
Aus den kälteren Himmeln fällt!

9

O himmlische Frucht der befleckten Empfängnis!
Was sahest du, Bruder, Vollkommnes allhier?
Man feiert mit Kirsch sich sein Leichenbegängnis
Und kleinen Laternen aus leichtem Papier.

10

Frühmorgens erwacht, auf haarigen Zähnen
Ein Grinsen sich find't zwischen faulem Tabak.
Auch finden wir oft auf der Zunge beim Gähnen
Einen bitterlichen Orangegeschmack.

6

One hands out the liquor, one hands out the coffee,
One drinks all the drinks, one drinks eau de cologne.
All this doesn't do it! Maria! We'd better
Start tanning some exquisite skins with snow!

7

With the cynical grace of frivolous poems
With a bitterness which has a faint orange taste
And which is ice-cooled! A Malayan hair-do
Waxed down on the forehead! O opium in

8

Wind-crazy cabins of fine Nanking paper!
O all the sad gladness of our little world
When the moon, that pallid and gentle monster,
Comes tumbling out of the colder skies!

9

O celestial fruit of a maculate conception,
Brother, what have you seen that is perfect down here?
One can celebrate here one's own funeral procession
With delicate small paper lanterns and kirsch.

10

And, waking up early, on teeth that are hairy
Midst the rotten tobacco we discover a grin.
Sometimes on the tongue we discover while yawning
A bitterness with a faint orange taste.

VOM KLETTERN IN BÄUMEN

1

Wenn ihr aus eurem Wasser steigt am Abend—
Denn ihr müßt nackt sein und die Haut muß weich sein—
Dann steigt auch noch auf eure großen Bäume
Bei leichtem Wind. Auch soll der Himmel bleich sein.
Sucht große Bäume, die am Abend schwarz
Und langsam ihre Wipfel wiegen, aus!
Und wartet auf die Nacht in ihrem Laub
Und um die Stirne Mahr und Fledermaus!

2

Die kleinen harten Blätter im Gesträuche
Zerkerben euch den Rücken, den ihr fest
Durchs Astwerk stemmen müßt; so klettert ihr
Ein wenig ächzend höher ins Geäst.
Es ist ganz schön, sich wiegen auf dem Baum!
Doch sollt ihr euch nicht wiegen mit den Knien!
Ihr sollt dem Baum so wie sein Wipfel sein:
Seit hundert Jahren abends: Er wiegt ihn.

ON CLIMBING IN TREES

1

And when you rise from water in the evening
(For you must all be naked, with soft skin)
Climb up your big trees while a very gentle
Wind blows; and the sky should be quite pale.
Seek out the bigger trees with tops that rock
Slowly and blackly in the evening air.
And in the foliage await the nightfall
With wraith and bat hovering about your brows.

2

The little leaves of the undergrowth are brittle.
They'll cut and scratch your backs which you must heave
Up through the branches; thus it is you clamber
Not without groaning, higher up the tree.
To rock oneself on the tree is quite delightful.
But do not flex your knees to do this! No,
Let the tree be to you what it is to the treetop:
Each evening, for centuries, it has rocked it.

VOM SCHWIMMEN IN SEEN UND FLÜSSEN

1

Im bleichen Sommer, wenn die Winde oben
Nur in dem Laub der großen Bäume sausen
Muß man in Flüssen liegen oder Teichen
Wie die Gewächse, worin Hechte hausen.
Der Leib wird leicht im Wasser. Wenn der Arm
Leicht aus dem Wasser in den Himmel fällt
Wiegt ihn der kleine Wind vergessen
Weil er ihn wohl für braunes Astwerk hält.

2

Der Himmel bietet mittags große Stille.
Man macht die Augen zu, wenn Schwalben kommen.
Der Schlamm ist warm. Wenn kühle Blasen quellen
Weiß man: ein Fisch ist jetzt durch uns geschwommen.
Mein Leib, die Schenkel und der stille Arm
Wir liegen still im Wasser, ganz geeint
Nur wenn die kühlen Fische durch uns schwimmen
Fühl ich, daß Sonne überm Tümpel scheint.

3

Wenn man am Abend von dem langen Liegen
Sehr faul wird, so, daß alle Glieder beißen
Muß man das alles, ohne Rücksicht, klatschend
in blaue Flüsse schmeißen, die sehr reißen.
Am besten ist's, man hält's bis Abend aus.
Weil dann der bleiche Haifischhimmel kommt
Bös und gefräßig über Fluß und Sträuchern
Und alle Dinge sind, wie's ihnen frommt.

ON SWIMMING IN LAKES AND RIVERS

1

In the pale summer when the winds are rustling
Only in the leaves of bigger trees
You must just lie in ponds or in the rivers
Like water-plants in which pike make their home.
The body grows light in water. And when your
Arm falls lightly from the water to the sky
The little wind will rock it quite oblivious
Because it takes it for brown foliage.

2

The sky at midday proffers a large stillness.
You shut your eyes up tight when swallows come.
The mud is warm. And when cool bubbles rise
You know a fish has just been swimming through us.
My two thighs and my still arm, my whole body,
We lie still in the water, all at one,
And only when the cool fish swim through us
Do I feel the sun is shining above the pool.

3

From all the lying comes by evening
A laziness. Your limbs begin to hurt.
The time has come to throw yourself regardless
And with a splash into the swift blue streams.
It's best if you remain there till the evening
For then above the bushes and the stream
Comes the pale shark sky, gluttonous and wicked
And everything is what it ought to be.

4

Natürlich muß man auf dem Rücken liegen
So wie gewöhnlich. Und sich treiben lassen.
Man muß nicht schwimmen, nein, nur so tun, als
Gehöre man einfach zu Schottermassen.
Man soll den Himmel anschaun und so tun
Als ob einen ein Weib trägt, und es stimmt.
Ganz ohne großen Umtrieb, wie der liebe Gott tut
Wenn er am Abend noch in seinen Flüssen schwimmt.

4

Of course you must lie flat upon your back,
As usual, and let yourself just float.
You must not swim, no, you must be as if you
Were a part of the earth like the gravel bed.
You should look up at the sky and act as if
A woman's womb still carried you: it fits:
And without fuss like the Lord God of an evening
When in His rivers He goes for a swim.

ORGES ANTWORT,
ALS IHM EIN GESEIFTER STRICK GESCHICKT WURDE

1

Oft sang er, es wäre ihm sehr recht
Wenn sein Leben besser wär:
Sein Leben sei tatsächlich sehr schlecht—
Jedoch sei es besser als er.

2

Strick und Seife nähme er gerne:
Es sei eine Schweinerei
Wie er auf diesem Sterne
Schmutzig geworden sei.

3

Doch gäbe es Höhen und Täler
Die man noch gar nie gesehn:
Es sei desto rentabler, je wähler-
ischer man sei im—Vorübergehn.

4

Solange die Sonne noch nah sei
Sei es noch nicht zu spät:
Und er warte, solang sie noch da sei
Und—solang sie noch untergeht.

5

Es blieben noch Bäume in Mengen
Schattig und durchaus kommun
Um oben sich aufzuhängen
Oder unten sich auszuruhn.

ORGE'S ANSWER
WHEN A SOAPED ROPE WAS SENT TO HIM*

1

If his life should improve, remarked Orge,
That would suit him, certainly.
For his life was quite bad, added Orge,
Yet his life was better than he.

2

So the rope and the soap were both welcome:
It's a shame, he'd have you know,
That by living on such a star he'd got
Filthy from top to toe.

3

And yet there were mountains and valleys
More indeed than one ever knew.
One got more from the whole thing the choosier
One showed oneself passing through.

4

And so long as the sun was still up there
So long it was not too late.
And he'd wait just as long as it stayed there
And as long as it took to set.

5

There were still splendid trees by the thousand
Inviting, shady, high.
You could hang yourself from a treetop
Or beneath a tree you could lie.

6

Jedoch seine letzte Realie
Gibt ein Mann nur ungern auf.
Ja, auf seine letzte Fäkalie
Legt er seine Hand darauf.

7

Erst wenn er von Ekel und Hasse
Voll bis zur Gurgel sei:
Schneide er sie, ohne Grimasse
Wahrscheinlich lässig, entzwei.

6

And as for one's last bit of real
Estate one holds on to it.
And one holds on with tooth and with nail to
Even one's last bit of shit.

7

And yet only when hate and disgust shall
Reach up to his throat will he
Cut that throat without any grimacing
And most likely nonchalantly.

BALLADE VON DEN GEHEIMNISSEN JEDWEDEN MANNES

1

Jeder weiß, was ein Mann ist. Er hat einen Namen.
Er geht auf der Straße. Er sitzt in der Bar.
Sein Gesicht könnt ihr sehn, seine Stimm
            könnt ihr hören
Und ein Weib wusch sein Hemd und ein Weib
            kämmt sein Haar.
Aber schlagt ihn tot, es ist nicht schad
Wenn er niemals mehr mit Haut und Haar
Als der Täter seiner Schandtat war
Und der Täter seiner guten Tat.

2

Und der Fleck ohne Haut auf der Brust, oh,
            den kennen
Sie auch und die Bisse an seinem Hals:
Die weiß, die sie biß und sie wird es dir sagen
Und der Mann, der die Haut hat: für den Fleck
            hat er Salz!
Aber salzt ihn ein, es ist nicht schad
Wenn er weint, o werft ihn auf den Mist!
Vor er euch schnell noch sagt, wer er ist.
Macht ihn stumm, wenn er um Schweigen bat!

3

Und doch hat er was auf dem Grund seines Herzens
Und das weiß kein Freund und nicht einmal sein Feind
Und sein Engel nicht und er selbst nicht und einstmals
Wenn ihr weint, wenn er stirbt: das ist's nicht,
            daß ihr weint.
Und vergeßt ihr ihn, es ist nicht schad

BALLAD OF THE SECRETS OF EACH AND EVERY MAN

1

Everyone knows what a man is. He has a name.
He walks in the street. He sits in the bar.
You can all see his face. You can all hear his voice
And a woman washed his shirt and a woman combs his hair.
But strike him dead! Why not indeed
If he never amounted to anything more
Than the doer of his bad deed or
The doer of his good deed?

2

And the skinless spot on his chest, they know that too!
And the bites on his neck, why, she who bit
Them knows, and will tell you so. The man
Who took the skin from the spot has salt for it.
But rub in the salt, and don't let him
Say who he is! If he should weep
O throw him on the garbage heap!
If he calls for silence, silence him!

3

And yet he has something in the depths of his heart
Which no friend knows nor enemy nor
His guardian angel nor himself and if one day
You're weeping at his death, *that's* not what you're weeping for.
Forget him! And why not indeed?
You are mistaken through and through.
He never was the one you knew.
He was not just the doer of his deed.

Denn ihr seid betrogen ganz und gar
Weil er niemals, den ihr kanntet, war
Und der Täter nicht nur seiner Tat.

4

Oh, der kindlich sein Brot mit den erdigen Händen
In die Zähne schiebt und es lachend zerkaut:
Die Tiere erbleichten vorm Haifischblicke
Dieser eigentümlichen Augapfelhaut!
Aber lacht mit ihm und seid ihm gut!
Laßt ihn leben, helft ihm etwas auf!
Ach, er ist nicht gut, verlaßt euch drauf
Doch ihr wißt nicht, was man euch noch tut!

5

Ihr, die ihr ihn werft in die schmutzgelben Meere
Ihr, die ihr in schwarze Erde ihn grabt:
In dem Sack schwimmt mehr, als ihr wißt,
                    zu den Fischen
Und im Boden fault mehr, als ihr eingescharrt habt.
Aber grabt nur ein, es ist nicht schad!
Denn das Gras, das er nicht einmal sah
Als er es zertrat, war nicht für Stiere da.
Und der Täter lebt nicht für die Tat!

4

See him throw his bread between his teeth with a child's dirty fingers!
Hear him laugh as he chews each morsel up, O hark!
The animals turned pale under the gaze
Of this extraordinary shark.
Laugh with him! Let him live—like you!
Get to like him! Help him out a bit!
He's worthless, there's no doubt of it.
But what after all is in store for you?

5

O you who throw him in the dirty yellow seas,
All you who in the black earth bury him,
More than you know floats down in that sack to the fishes,
And more rots in the ground than you shoveled in.
But bury him! Why not indeed?
The grass he didn't notice as his feet
Trod it down wasn't there for steers to eat.
And the doer does not live for the deed!

LIED AM SCHWARZEN SAMSTAG IN DER ELFTEN STUNDE
DER NACHT VOR OSTERN

1

Im Frühjahr unter grünen Himmeln, wilden
Verliebten Winden schon etwas vertiert
Fuhr ich hinunter in die schwarzen Städte
Mit kalten Sprüchen innen tapeziert.

2

Ich füllte mich mit schwarzen Asphalttieren
Ich füllte mich mit Wasser und Geschrei
Mich aber ließ es kalt und leicht, mein Lieber
Ich bleib ganz ungefüllt und leicht dabei.

3

Sie schlugen Löcher wohl in meine Wände
Und krochen fluchend wieder aus von mir:
Es war nichts drinnen als viel Platz und Stille
Sie schrieen fluchend: ich sei nur Papier.

4

Ich rollte feixend abwärts zwischen Häusern
Hinaus ins Freie. Leis und feierlich
Lief jetzt der Wind schneller durch meine Wände
Es schneite noch. Es regnete in mich.

5

Zynischer Burschen arme Rüssel haben
Gefunden, daß in mir nichts ist.

SONG ON BLACK SATURDAY AT THE ELEVENTH HOUR OF
THE NIGHT BEFORE EASTER

1

In spring beneath green heavens by belovèd
And savage winds a little brutalized
Down to the black cities I came rolling,
A lining of cold sayings in my heart.

2

I filled myself with black beasts of the pavements
I filled myself with water and with cries.
They left me cold, they left me light, my hearties!
I stayed unfilled, I stayed quite light, throughout.

3

And they knocked holes right through my walls, I know it.
Then, cursing, they crept out of me again.
Nothing inside me but much space and silence!
I was mere paper—so they, cursing, cried.

4

And smirking I rolled down between the houses
Into the open country. Festive, soft.
The wind now ran through all my walls more quickly.
And snow fell still. The rain rained into me.

5

Poor snouts of cynic bully-boys discovered
In me there's nothing—absolutely nix!

Wildsäue haben sich in mir begattet. Raben
Des milchigen Himmels oft in mich gepißt.

6

Schwächer als Wolken! Leichter als die Winde!
Nicht sichbar! Leicht, vertiert und feierlich
Wie ein Gedicht von mir, flog ich durch Himmel
Mit einem Storch, der etwas schneller strich!

Wild pigs paired in me. From the milky heavens
The ravens often pissed right into me.

6

Weaker than clouds! And lighter than the winds are!
Not visible, but brutal, festive, light
As one of my own poems, I crossed the heavens
With a stork, whose wings beat faster, at my side!

GROSSER DANKCHORAL

1

Lobet die Nacht und die Finsternis, die euch
    umfangen!
Kommet zuhauf
Schaut in den Himmel hinauf:
Schon ist der Tag euch vergangen.

2

Lobet das Gras und die Tiere, die neben euch
    leben und sterben!
Sehet, wie ihr
Lebet das Gras und das Tier
Und es muß auch mit euch sterben.

3

Lobet den Baum, der aus Aas aufwächst jauch-
    zend zum Himmel!
Lobet das Aas
Lobet den Baum, der es fraß
Aber auch lobet den Himmel.

4

Lobet von Herzen das schlechte Gedächtnis des
    Himmels!
Und daß er nicht
Weiß euren Nam' noch Gesicht
Niemand weiß, daß ihr noch da seid.

GRAND HYMN OF THANKSGIVING

1

Praise ye the night and the darkness
        of night all around you!
All ye, come nigh!
Look at the Heavens on high!
Your day is already over.

2

Praise ye the grass and the beasts that
        both live and die with you!
And see how the
Grass and beasts live as do ye
And how they die just as you will.

3

Praise ye the tree that from carrion shoots
        whooping toward Heaven!
Praise ye the tree!
Carrion that feeds it, praise ye!
But never cease to praise Heaven.

4

Rejoice that Heaven above us has such a bad
        memory
And cannot place
Either your name or your face.
No one knows you are still living.

5

Lobet die Kälte, die Finsternis und das Verderben!
Schauet hinan:
Es kommet nicht auf euch an
Und ihr könnt unbesorgt sterben.

5
Praise ye the coldness, the darkness,
     the disintegration!
Wake up and sing:
You do not count for a thing
And without qualms you can perish.

DRITTE LEKTION

Chroniken

THIRD LESSON

Chronicles

BALLADE VON DEN ABENTEURERN

1

Von Sonne krank und ganz von Regen zerfressen
Geraubten Lorbeer im zerrauften Haar
Hat er seine ganze Jugend, nur nicht ihre Träume vergessen
Lange das Dach, nie den Himmel, der drüber war.

2

O ihr, die ihr aus Himmel und Hölle vertrieben
Ihr Mörder, denen viel Leides geschah
Warum seid ihr nicht im Schoß eurer Mütter geblieben
Wo es stille war und man schlief und man war da?

3

Er aber sucht noch in absinthenen Meeren
Wenn ihn schon seine Mutter vergißt
Grinsend und fluchend und zuweilen nicht ohne Zähren
Immer das Land, so es besser zu leben ist.

4

Schlendernd durch Höllen und gepeitscht durch Paradiese
Still und grinsend vergehenden Gesichts
Träumt er gelegentlich von einer kleinen Wiese
Mit blauem Himmel drüber und sonst nichts.

BALLAD OF THE ADVENTURERS*

1

Sick from the sun, and gnawed at by the rainstorms,
With stolen laurels in his tousled hair
He forgot his childhood, except for childhood's daydreams,
Forgot the roof but never the sky above.

2

You who were banished out of hell and heaven
You murderers whose lot is pain and woe
Why did you not stay inside the wombs of your mothers
Where it was calm and one slumbered and one was?

3

But now that even his mother has forgot him
He still is seeking in the absinthe seas
Grinning and cursing and from time to time weeping
The country where there is a better life.

4

Strolling through hells and whipped through paradises
A grin upon his calm and fading face
He dreams at times about a little meadow
A patch of blue in the sky and nothing more.

BALLADE AUF VIELEN SCHIFFEN

1

Brackwasser ist braun und die alten Schaluppen
Liegen dick und krebsig darin herum.
Mit Laken, einst weiß, jetzt wie kotige Hemden
Am verkommenen Mast, der verfault ist und krumm.
Die Wassersucht treibt die verschwammten Leiber
Sie wissen nicht mehr, wie das Segeln tut.
Bei Mondlicht und Wind, Aborte der Möven
Schaukeln sie faul auf der Salzwasserflut.

2

Wer alles verließ sie? Es ziemt nicht zu zählen
Jedenfalls sind sie fort und ihr Kaufbrief verjährt
Doch kommt es noch vor, daß einer sich findet
Der nach nichts mehr fragt und auf ihnen fährt.
Er hat keinen Hut, er kommt nackt geschwommen
Er hat kein Gesicht mehr, er hat zuviel Haut!
Selbst dies Schiff erschauert noch vor seinem Grinsen
Wenn er von oben seiner Spur im Kielwasser nachschaut.

3

Denn er ist nicht alleine gekommen
Aus dem Himmel nicht, Haie hat er dabei!
Haie sind mit ihm den Weg hergeschwommen
Und sie wohnen bei ihm, wo immer er sei.
So stellt er sich ein, der letzte Verführer
So finden sie sich im Vormittagslicht
Und von andern Schiffen löst schwankend sich ein Schiff
Das vor Angst Wasser läßt und vor Reu Salz erbricht.

BALLAD ABOARD MANY SHIPS

1

Brackish water is brown and the ancient sloops
Lie around in the water, cancerous and swollen
With sails, once white, but now like crappy shirts
On the ruined mast which is bent and rotten.
The spongy bodies are driven by dropsy.
They have forgotten what it is to sail.
By moonlight and in the wind (the seagulls' privy)
The rotten ships rock on the salty swell.

2

And who has left them? It is no use counting!
Their contract has expired, and so goodbye!
And yet it happens there's one man around
Who'll sail, on these ships even, and not ask why.
He has no hat. Swimming he comes and naked.
He has no face left. He has too much skin.
He looks down at the water in its wake
And even this ship shudders at his grin.

3

Because he did not come this way alone
Or from the sky. He has got sharks in tow.
He comes this way accompanied by sharks:
They live with him wherever he may go.
He has arrived here then: the last seducer.
And gathering in the morning sun, they're here.
A ship breaks loose from other ships. It vomits
Salt in remorse. It makes water in fear.

4

Er schneidet sein letztes Segel zur Jacke
Er schöpft seinen Mittagsfisch aus der See
Er liegt in der Sonne und badet am Abend
In des Schiffsrumpfs Wasser reinlich seinen Zeh.
Mitunter schauend zum milchigen Himmel
Gewahrt er Möven. Die fängt er mit Schlingen aus Tang.
Mit denen füttert er abends die Haie
Und vertröstet sie so manche Woche lang.

5

Oh, während er kreuzt in den Ostpassatwinden
Liegt er in den Tauen: verfaulend ein Aal
Und die Haie hören ihn oft einen Song singen
Und sie sagen: er singt einen Song am Marterpfahl.
Doch an einem Abend im Monat Oktober
Nach einem Tage ohne Gesang
Erscheint er am Heck und sie hören ihn reden
Und was sagt er? ,,Morgen ist Untergang.“

6

Und in folgender Nacht, er liegt in den Tauen
Er liegt und er schläft; denn er ist es gewohnt
Da fühlt er: ein neues Schiff ist gekommen
Und er schaut hinab und da liegt es im Mond.
Und er nimmt sich ein Herz und steigt grinsend hinüber
Er schaut sich nicht um, er kämmt sich sein Haar
Daß er schön ist. Was macht es, daß diese Geliebte
Schlechter als jene Geliebte war?

7

Ach, er steht noch einige Zeit an der Bordwand
Und schaut, und es ist ihm vergönnt zu schaun

4

He cuts himself a coat from its last sail.
He scoops a fish for dinner from the sea.
He lies in the sun, at evening bathes his toes
In water from the hull fastidiously.
Looking on and off at the milky sky
He bags some seagulls with a seaweed sling,
And with them feeds the sharks for many weeks
Getting their hopes up thus each evening.

5

While they were cruising in the Eastern trade winds
Among the ropes, roasting and rotting, he lay.
The sharks quite often heard him sing a song.
"He is singing a song at the stake!" is what they say.
But one evening in the fall—it was October—
After a day on which there was no singing
He appears at the stern and they hear him speak.
And what he says is "Tomorrow we'll be sinking."

6

That night when he is sleeping in the ropes—
For he can sleep since he's so used to it—
And he feels in his heart that a new ship has come.
He looks down. There in the moonlight—a ship!
And he takes heart and goes to the other boat.
He combs his hair so it looks good. He's bold
And does not look around. What matter if
The new girl friend is worse than the old?

7

Oh, he stands a little while at the rail
And sees—it's granted him to see—how the ship

Wie das Schiff jetzt sinkt, das ihm Heimat und Bett war
Und er sieht ein paar Haie zwischen den Tauen . . .

8
So lebt er weiter, den Wind in den Augen
Auf immer schlechteren Schiffen fort
Auf vielen Schiffen, schon halb im Wasser
und mondweis wechselt er seinen Abort.
Ohne Hut und nackt und mit eigenen Haien.
Er kennt seine Welt. Er hat sie gesehn.
Er hat eine Lust in sich: zu versaufen
Und er hat eine Lust: nicht unterzugehn.

Which has been his bed, his home, now sinks at once
And he catches sight of a couple of sharks in the ropes. . . .

8

And thus on many ships, one worse than the other,
With the wind in his face he sails night, morning, noon,
On many ships already half under water
Changing his privy as moon gives place to moon,
Naked and with his sharks and without a hat.
He knows his world. He has looked into that.
And he has one desire left: to drown.
And he has one desire: not to go down.

VOM TOD IM WALD

1

Und ein Mann starb im Hathourywald
Wo der Mississippi brauste.
Starb wie ein Tier in Wurzeln eingekrallt
Schaute hoch in die Wipfel, wo über den Wald
Sturm seit Tagen ohne Aufhörn sauste.

2

Und es standen einige um ihn
Und sie sagten, daß er stiller werde:
Komm, wir tragen dich jetzt heim, Gefährte.
Aber er stieß sie mit seinen Knien
Spuckte aus und sagte: und wohin?
Denn er hatte weder Heim noch Erde.

3

Wieviel Zähne hast du noch im Maul?
Und wie ist das sonst mit dir, laß sehn!
Stirb ein wenig ruhiger und nicht so faul!
Gestern abend aßen wir schon deinen Gaul
Warum willst du nicht zur Hölle gehn?

4

Denn der Wald war laut um ihn und sie
Und sie sahn: ihn sich am Baume halten
Und sie hörten: wie er ihnen schrie.
Rauchend standen sie im Wald von Hathoury
Und mit Ärger sahn sie ihn erkalten
Denn er war ein Mann wie sie.

ON THE DEATH IN THE FOREST

1

And a man died in the Hathoury forest
Where the Mississippi was roaring
Died like a beast with its claws in the roots
Looked high into the treetops where over the forest
For days the storm was raging.

2

And several men were standing by
And they said, to calm him down:
Come on, we'll take you home now, comrade.
But he kicked them with his knees
And spat and said: Where?
For he had neither home nor land.

3

How many teeth left in that snout of yours?
How are things with you otherwise? Let's see.
Die a bit more calmly, and make it snappy!
We ate your horse last night already
So why don't you want to go to hell?

4

For the forest was loud around them and him
And they saw how he clung to the tree
And they heard how he cried out to them.
They stood in the Hathoury forest smoking
And saw him grow cold with some annoyance for
He was a man like them.

5

Du benimmst dich schäbig wie ein Tier!
Sei ein Gentleman, kein Elendshaufen!
Ja, was ist denn das mit dir?
Und er sah sie an, kaputt vor Gier:
Leben will ich! Essen! Faul sein! Schnaufen!
Und im Wind fortreiten so wie ihr!

6

Das war etwas, was kein Freund verstand:
Dreimal riefen sie mit Gentleman ihn an.
Dreimal lachte da der vierte Mann:
Ihm hielt Erde seine nackte Hand
Als er krebsig lag im schwarzen Tann.

7

Als ihn dann der Wald von Hathoury fraß
Gruben sie den sehr vom Tau Durchnäßten
Noch am Morgen durch das dunkle Gras
Voll von Ekel noch und kalt von Haß
In des Baumes unterstes Geäste.

8

Und sie ritten stumm aus dem Dickicht
Und sie sahn noch nach dem Baume hin
Unter den sie eingegraben ihn
Dem das Sterben allzu bitter schien:
Und der Baum war oben voll Licht.
Und sie bekreuzten ihr junges Gesicht
Und sie ritten schnell in die Prärien.

5

The way you behave! A beast could do better!
Be a gentleman, not a pile of self-pity!
What *is* the matter with you, huh?
Knocked out by desire, he looked at them:
I want to live! To eat, breathe, and be lazy!
I want to ride off in the wind like you!

6

That was something that no friend understood
And three times over they called him "gentleman."
Three times over the fourth man laughed:
The earth took him by the naked hand
As, cancerous, he lay amid the black fir branches.

7

And when thereupon the Hathoury forest devoured him
Soaked with dew as he was they dug him down
Through the dark grass on the same morning
Full of disgust as they were and cold with hate
Beneath the lowest branches of the tree.

8

And they rode without a word out of the thicket
And looked once again toward the tree
Under which they had buried him
To whom death seemed all too bitter:
And the tree, up above, was full of light.
And they crossed their young faces
And rode swiftly out on to the prairies.

DAS LIED VON DER EISENBAHNTRUPPE
VON FORT DONALD

1

Die Männer von Fort Donald—hohé!
Zogen den Strom hinauf, bis die Wälder ewig und
seelenlos sind.
Aber eines Tages ging Regen nieder und der Wald
wuchs um sie zum See.
Sie standen im Wasser bis an die Knie.
Und der Morgen kommt nie, sagten sie
Und wir versaufen vor der Früh, sagten sie
Und sie horchten stumm auf den Eriewind.

2

Die Männer von Fort Donald—hohé!
Standen am Wasser mit Pickel und Schiene und schauten
zum dunkleren Himmel hinauf
Denn es ward dunkel und Abend wuchs aus dem
plätschernden See.
Ach, kein Fetzen Himmel, der Hoffnung lieh
Und wir sind schon müd, sagten sie
Und wir schlafen noch ein, sagten sie
Und uns weckt keine Sonne mehr auf.

3

Die Männer von Fort Donald—hohé!
Sagten gleich: wenn wir einschlafen, sind wir adje!
Denn Schlaf wuchs aus Wasser und Nacht, und sie
waren voll Furcht wie Vieh
Einer sagte: singt „Johnny über der See".
Ja, das hält uns vielleicht auf, sagten sie

THE SONG OF THE FORT DONALD RAILROAD GANG

1

The men of Fort Donald, yo-ho!
Upstream they went where the forests
    are soulless and everlasting.
But one day rain fell and the forest
    rose around them in a lake.
The water came up to their knees.
And tomorrow will not come, said they
We shall drown before dawn, said they
Silent, they listened to the wind from Erie.

2

The men of Fort Donald, yo-ho!
Stood in the water with pick and rail,
    and looked up at the darker sky
For it got dark and evening rose out
    of the rippling lake.
No patch of clear sky offered hope.
And we're tired already, said they
And we're falling asleep, said they
No sun will ever wake us up again.

3

The men of Fort Donald, yo-ho!
Right away said: If we doze off,
    it's goodbye!
For sleep rose from water and night,
    and they were full of fear like cattle.
One of them said: Sing "Johnny over the sea."
That may keep us on our feet, said they

Ja, wir singen seinen Song, sagten sie
Und sie sangen von Johnny über der See.

4

Die Männer von Fort Donald—hohé!
Tappten in diesem dunklen Ohio wie Maulwürfe blind
Aber sie sangen so laut, als ob ihnen wunder was
     Angenehmes geschäh
Ja, so sangen sie nie.
Oh, wo ist mein Johnny zur Nacht, sangen sie
Oh, wo ist mein Johnny zur Nacht, sangen sie
Und das nasse Ohio wuchts unten, und oben
     wuchs Regen und Wind.

5

Die Männer von Fort Donald—hohé!
Werden jetzt wachen und singen, bis sie ersoffen sind.
Doch das Wasser ist höher als sie bis zur Früh und
     lauter als sie der Eriewind schrie
Wo ist mein Johnny zur Nacht, sangen sie
Dieses Ohio ist naß, sagten sie
Früh wachte nur noch das Wasser und nur noch
     der Eriewind.

6

Die Männer von Fort Donald—hohé!
Die Züge sausen über sie weg an den Eriesee
Und der Wind an der Stelle singt eine dumme Melodie
Und die Kiefern schrein den Zügen nach: hohé!
Damals kam der Morgen nie, schreien sie
Ja, sie versoffen vor der Früh, schreien sie
Unser Wind singt abends oft noch
     ihren Johnny über der See.

We will sing his song, said they
And they sang of Johnny over the sea.

4

The men of Fort Donald, yo-ho!
Groped their way in this dark Ohio
    blindly like moles.
Loudly they sang as if God-knows-
    what-nice-thing had happened.
Never had they sung so.
Oh, where is my Johnny at night, sang they
Oh, where is my Johnny at night, sang they
And below them rose this wet Ohio while
    above them rose rain and wind.

5

The men of Fort Donald, yo-ho!
Will wake now and sing till they drown.
But by dawn the water is higher than they
    and the wind from Erie screams louder than they.
Where is my Johnny at night, sang they
This Ohio is wet, sang they
But only the water woke at dawn, only the
    wind from Erie.

6

The men of Fort Donald, yo-ho!
The trains whistle over them and on to Lake Erie
And the wind sings a stupid tune at that spot
And the pines scream after the trains: yo-ho!
Morning did not come that time, scream they
Yes, they were drowned before dawn, scream they
Often of an evening our wind still sings
    their "Johnny over the sea."

BALLADE VON DES CORTEZ LEUTEN

Am siebten Tage unter leichten Winden
Wurden die Wiesen heller. Da die Sonne gut war
Gedachten sie zu rasten. Rollen Branntwein
Von den Gefährten, koppeln Ochsen los.
Die schlachten sie gen Abend. Als es kühl ward
Schlug man vom Holz des nachbarlichen Sumpfes
Armdicke Äste, knorrig, gut zu brennen.
Dann schlingen sie gewürztes Fleisch hinunter
Und fangen singend um die neunte Stunde
Mit Trinken an. Die Nacht war kühl und grün.
Mit heisrer Kehle, tüchtig vollgesogen
Mit einem letzten, kühlen Blick nach großen Sternen
Entschliefen sie gen Mitternacht am Feuer.
Sie schlafen schwer, doch mancher wußte morgens
Daß er die Ochsen einmal brüllen hörte.
Erwacht gen Mittag, sind sie schon im Wald.
Mit glasigen Augen, schweren Gliedern, heben
Sie ächzend sich aufs Knie und sehen staunend
Armdicke Äste, knorrig, um sie stehen
Höher als mannshoch, sehr verwirrt, mit Blattwerk
Und kleinen Blüten süßlichen Geruchs.
Es ist sehr schwül schon unter ihrem Dach
Das sich zu dichten scheint. Die heiße Sonne
Ist nicht zu sehen, auch der Himmel nicht.
Der Hauptmann brüllte wie ein Stier nach Äxten.
Die lagen drüben, wo die Ochsen brüllten.
Man sah sie nicht. Mit rauhem Fluchen stolpern
Die Leute im Geviert, ans Astwerk stoßend
Das zwischen ihnen durchgekrochen war.
Mit schlaffen Armen werfen sie sich wild
In die Gewächse, die leicht zitterten
Als ginge leichter Wind von außen durch sie.
Nach Stunden Arbeit pressen sie die Stirnen

BALLAD OF CORTEZ' MEN

It was the seventh day and light winds blew.
The meadows grew lighter. There was a good
Sun and they thought to rest. From carts they rolled
Their brandy and uncoupled some of the oxen.
They slaughtered these toward evening. And when it
Grew cool they cut from the wood of the neighboring swamp
Some boughs, arm-thick and knotted, good for burning.
Then they wolf down some spiced meat and, singing, start
To drink. The hour now is nine. The night is cool
And green. With hoarse throats, loaded with good liquor,
And taking one last cool look at the great stars
Toward midnight they fall asleep by their fire.
They sleep heavily. But many knew in the morning
That they had heard their oxen bellowing.
Wakened toward noon, they find themselves in a forest.
With glassy eyes and heavy limbs they rise
To their knees and see with astonishment
Branches, arm-thick and knotted, all around them,
Taller than men are, very tangled, and with
Foliage and little flowers that smell sweet.
It's very sultry now beneath this roof
Which, seemingly, gets thicker. The hot sun
Cannot be seen, nor can the sky above it.
The captain bellowed like a steer for axes
And these lay yonder where the oxen bellowed.
They could not see them. With coarse cursing they
Stagger through the camp colliding with the
Tangle of brushwork that shot up among them.
Now with limp arms they furiously throw
Themselves at all these plants which slightly quivered
As if a light wind blew through them from outside.
After hours of work, they darkly press their foreheads
Gleaming with sweat against the alien boughs.

Schweißglänzend finster an die fremden Äste.
Die Äste wuchsen und vermehrten langsam
Das schreckliche Gewirr. Später, am Abend
Der dunkler war, weil oben Blattwerk wuchs
Sitzen sie schweigend, angstvoll und wie Affen
In ihren Käfigen, von Hunger matt.
Nachts wuchs das Astwerk. Doch es mußte Mond sein
Es war noch ziemlich hell, sie sahn sich noch.
Erst gegen Morgen war das Zeug so dick
Daß sie sich nimmer sahen, bis sie starben.
Den nächsten Tag stieg Singen aus dem Wald.
Dumpf und verhallt. Sie sangen sich wohl zu.
Nachts ward es stiller. Auch die Ochsen schwiegen.
Gen Morgen war es, als ob Tiere brüllten
Doch ziemlich weit weg. Später kamen Stunden
Wo es ganz still war. Langsam fraß der Wald
In leichtem Wind, bei guter Sonne, still
Die Wiesen in den nächsten Wochen auf.

The branches grew and steadily increased
The terrible tangle. Later, in the evening,
Which was darker because foliage grew on top,
They sit there silent, fearful and like apes
In their cages, done up with hunger. At night
The branches grew. But there must have been a moon:
It was rather light and they could see one another.
Only toward morning was the stuff so thick
That they would never see one another again.
Next day a sound of singing rose from the woods
Hollow and dull. They were singing for one another.
The night was quieter. Even the oxen were silent.
And toward the morning it was just as if
The cattle bellowed dimly and at a distance.
Later came hours of stillness. Quiet, slow,
Beneath a good sun and while light winds blew
The forest ate the meadows up in a matter of weeks.

BALLADE VON DEN SEERÄUBERN

1

Von Branntwein toll und Finsternissen!
Von unerhörten Güssen naß!
Vom Frost eisweißer Nacht zerrissen!
Im Mastkorb, von Gesichten blaß!
Von Sonne nackt gebrannt und krank!
(Die hatten sie im Winter lieb)
Aus Hunger, Fieber und Gestank
Sang alles, was noch übrig blieb:
O Himmel, strahlender Azur!
Enormer Wind, die Segel bläh!
Laßt Wind und Himmel fahren! Nur
Laßt uns um Sankt Marie die See!

2

Kein Weizenfeld mit milden Winden
Selbst keine Schenke mit Musik
Kein Tanz mit Weibern und Absinthen
Kein Kartenspiel hielt sie zurück.
Sie hatten vor dem Knall das Zanken
Vor Mitternacht die Weiber satt:
Sie lieben nur verfaulte Planken
Ihr Schiff, das keine Heimat hat.
O Himmel, strahlender Azur!
Enormer Wind, die Segel bläh!
Laßt Wind und Himmel fahren! Nur
Laßt uns um Sankt Marie die See!

3

Mit seinen Ratten, seinen Löchern
Mit seiner Pest, mit Haut und Haar

BALLAD OF THE PIRATES

1

Deranged by drink and all the darkness
Mangled by frost in icy night
Drenched by the rains, high in the crow's nest
They all saw visions and turned white.
Naked and sick, burnt by a sun which
In winter they wished back again
In scorching fever, stench, and hunger,
Those who survived sang this refrain:
Stare on, O sky of streaming blue!
Do, wind, the worst that you can do!
To hell with sky and wind if we
Command the seas round Saint Marie!

2

No cornfield with its gentle breezes
No music in no drinking den
No dance with girls, mid absinthe glasses,
No card game could hold back these men.
They tire of brawls before the morning
Even from girls their thoughts will roam
Their only love the rotten planks of
This pirate ship which has no home.
Stare on, O sky of streaming blue!
Do, wind, the worst that you can do!
To hell with sky and wind if we
Command the seas round Saint Marie!

3

With all its holes and its diseases
With all its rats, they'd damn its eyes

Sie fluchten wüst darauf beim Bechern
Und liebten es, so wie es war.
Sie knoten sich mit ihren Haaren
Im Sturm in seinem Mastwerk fest:
Sie würden nur zum Himmel fahren
Wenn man dort Schiffe fahren läßt.
O Himmel, strahlender Azur!
Enormer Wind, die Segel bläh!
Laßt Wind und Himmel fahren! Nur
Laßt uns um Sankt Marie die See!

4

Sie häufen Seide, schöne Steine
Und Gold in ihr verfaultes Holz
Sie sind auf die geraubten Weine
In ihren wüsten Mägen stolz.
Um dürren Leib riecht toter Dschunken
Seide glühbunt nach Prozession
Doch sie zerstechen sich betrunken
Im Zank um einen Lampion.
O Himmel, strahlender Azur!
Enormer Wind, die Segel bläh!
Laßt Wind und Himmel fahren! Nur
Laßt uns um Sankt Marie die See!

5

Sie morden kalt und ohne Hassen
Was ihnen in die Zähne springt
Sie würgen Gurgeln so gelassen
Wie man ein Tau ins Mastwerk schlingt.
Sie trinken Sprit bei Leichenwachen
Nachts torkeln trunken sie in See
Und die, die übrig bleiben, lachen
Und winken mit der kleinen Zeh:

And curse it with their drunken curses
Yet would not wish it otherwise.
And in a storm they'd tie themselves to
The rigging by their own long hair.
Even to heaven they would go if
They were allowed to sail ships there.
Stare on, O sky of streaming blue!
Do, wind, the worst that you can do!
To hell with sky and wind if we
Command the seas round Saint Marie!

4

They heap up silk, gold, precious jewels
All in that rotten hulk's inside
And in the wine that they have stolen
(Dead drunk by now) take proper pride.
The colored silk of dead old junks on
Their hard backs smelled of pageantry
Though in a fight about a lantern
They stab each other drunkenly.
Stare on, O sky of streaming blue!
Do, wind, the worst that you can do!
To hell with sky and wind if we
Command the seas round Saint Marie!

5

They murder coldly with no hatred
And what obstructs their teeth must rot.
They'll wring some gurgling epiglottis
As one might tie a double knot.
At many a wake, drunk on crude spirits,
Cavorting in the sea they go.
Those left behind all burst out laughing
And beckon with their little toe.

O Himmel, strahlender Azur!
Enormer Wind, die Segel bläh!
Laßt Wind und Himmel fahren! Nur
Laßt uns um Sankt Marie die See!

6

Vor violetten Horizonten
Still unter bleichem Mond im Eis
Bei schwarzer Nacht in Frühjahrsmonden
Wo keiner von dem andern weiß
Sie lauern wolfgleich in den Sparren
Und treiben funkeläugig Mord
Und singen um nicht zu erstarren
Wie Kinder, trommelnd im Abort:
O Himmel, strahlender Azur!
Enormer Wind, die Segel bläh!
Laßt Wind und Himmel fahren! Nur
Laßt uns um Sankt Marie die See!

7

Sie tragen ihren Bauch zum Fressen
Auf fremde Schiffe wie nach Haus
Und strecken selig im Vergessen
Ihn auf die fremden Frauen aus.
Sie leben schön wie noble Tiere
Im weichen Wind, im trunknen Blau!
Und oft besteigen sieben Stiere
Eine geraubte fremde Frau.
O Himmel, strahlender Azur!
Enormer Wind, die Segel bläh!
Laßt Wind und Himmel fahren! Nur
Laßt uns um Sankt Marie die See!

Stare on, O sky of streaming blue!
Do, wind, the worst that you can do!
To hell with sky and wind if we
Command the seas round Saint Marie!

6

Confronting violet horizons
Calm under pallid moons, in ice,
In the black nights of early springtime
When none can see his brother's face
They lurk like wolves high in the rafters.
Their eyes flash as they kill their man.
So as not to freeze, they sing like children
Making a racket in the john:
Stare on, O sky of streaming blue!
Do, wind, the worst that you can do!
To hell with sky and wind if we
Command the seas round Saint Marie!

7

They take their bellies and they fill them
On strangers' ships as on their own
And stretch out on the strangers' women
Ecstatic in oblivion.
The sky is drunk, the wind is gentle,
They live like splendid animals.
A single, stolen, stranger woman
Is often mounted by six bulls.
Stare on, O sky of streaming blue!
Do, wind, the worst that you can do!
To hell with sky and wind if we
Command the seas round Saint Marie!

8

Wenn man viel Tanz in müden Beinen
Und Sprit in satten Bäuchen hat
Mag Mond und zugleich Sonne scheinen:
Man hat Gesang und Messer satt.
Die hellen Sternennächte schaukeln
Sie mit Musik in süße Ruh
Und mit geblähten Segeln gaukeln
Sie unbekannten Meeren zu.
O Himmel, strahlender Azur!
Enormer Wind, die Segel bläh!
Laßt Wind und Himmel fahren! Nur
Laßt uns um Sankt Marie die See!

9

Doch eines Abends im Aprile
Der keine Sterne für sie hat
Hat sie das Meer in aller Stille
Auf einmal plötzlich selber satt.
Der große Himmel, den sie lieben
Hüllt still in Rauch die Sternensicht
Und die geliebten Winde schieben
Die Wolken in das milde Licht.
O Himmel, strahlender Azur!
Enormer Wind, die Segel bläh!
Laßt Wind und Himmel fahren! Nur
Laßt uns um Sankt Marie die See!

10

Der leichte Wind des Mittags fächelt
Sie anfangs spielend in die Nacht
Und der Azur des Abends lächelt
Noch einmal über schwarzem Schacht.
Sie fühlen noch, wie voll Erbarmen

8

And when their legs are tired of dancing
And tippling has gone on too long
Though sun and moon should shine together
They've had their fill of knife and song.
The bright and starry nights will rock them
To sleep with sweetest melodies
And then will fill the sails and steer them
Away to the uncharted seas.
Stare on, O sky of streaming blue!
Do, wind, the worst that you can do!
To hell with sky and wind if we
Command the seas round Saint Marie!

9

And yet one evening—it was April
And no star in the sky for them—
All of a sudden in the stillness
The sea had had enough of them.
The sky they love is full of vapor
That hides the shining stars from sight.
The winds they love propel the clouds which
Float gently on toward the light.
Stare on, O sky of streaming blue!
Do, wind, the worst that you can do!
To hell with sky and wind if we
Command the seas round Saint Marie!

10

At first the placid wind of morning
Fans them toward night a little bit
And then the azure of the evening
Half smiles above the pitch-black pit.
They think the sea, full of compassion,

Das Meer mit ihnen heute wacht
Dann nimmt der Wind sie in die Arme
Und tötet sie vor Mitternacht.
O Himmel, strahlender Azur!
Enormer Wind, die Segel bläh!
Laßt Wind und Himmel fahren! Nur
Laßt uns um Sankt Marie die See!

11

Noch einmal schmeißt die letzte Welle
Zum Himmel das verfluchte Schiff
Und da, in ihrer letzten Helle
Erkennen sie das große Riff.
Und ganz zuletzt in höchsten Masten
War es, weil Sturm so gar laut schrie
Als ob sie, die zur Hölle rasten
Noch einmal sangen, laut wie nie:
O Himmel, strahlender Azur!
Enormer Wind, die Segel bläh!
Laßt Wind und Himmel fahren! Nur
Laßt uns um Sankt Marie die See!

Is keeping watch now like themselves.
Then in its arms the sea wind takes them
And kills them ere the stroke of twelve.
Stare on, O sky of streaming blue!
Do, wind, the worst that you can do!
To hell with sky and wind if we
Command the seas round Saint Marie!

11

The last wave throws the accursed vessel
Toward the sky—O respite brief!
In this their last illumination
They recognize the final reef.
And in the end, atop the masthead,
Amid the tempest's dreadful roar
It seemed that on their way to hell they
Sang even louder than before:
Stare on, O sky of streaming blue!
Do, wind, the worst that you can do!
To hell with sky and wind if we
Command the seas round Saint Marie!

LIED DER DREI SOLDATEN

1

George war darunter und John war dabei
Und Freddy ist Sergeant geworden.
Und die Armee, sie zeigt, wer sie sei
Und marschierte hinauf in den Norden.

2

Freddy war der Whisky zu warm
Und George hatte nie genug Decken.
Aber Johnny nimmt Georgie beim Arm
Und sagt: die Armee kann nicht verrecken.

3

George ist gefallen und Freddy ist tot
Und Johnny vermißt und verdorben.
Aber Blut ist immer noch rot
Und für die Armee wird jetzt wieder geworben.

SONG OF THE THREE SOLDIERS

1

George was around, and John was too,
And Fred became a sergeant in short order.
And the army, to show what it could do,
Marched northward to the border.

2

And Freddy found the whisky warm
And George at night would shake and shiver
But John said as he took George by the arm:
Remember that the army lives forever!

3

Now George has fallen and Fred is dead
And John got lost in the shooting.
Blood, however, is still blood-red
And the army is again recruiting.

BALLADE VON DER HANNA CASH

1

Mit dem Rock von Kattun und dem gelben Tuch
Und den Augen der schwarzen Seen
Ohne Geld und Talent und doch mit genug
Vom Schwarzhaar, das sie offen trug
Bis zu den schwärzeren Zeh'n:
Das war die Hanna Cash, mein Kind
Die die ,,Gentlemen" eingeseift
Die kam mit dem Wind und ging mit dem Wind
Der in die Savannen läuft.

2

Die hatte keine Schuhe und die hatte auch kein Hemd
Und die konnte auch keine Choräle!
Und sie war wie eine Katze in die große Stadt geschwemmt
Eine kleine graue Katze zwischen Hölzer eingeklemmt
Zwischen Leichen in die schwarzen Kanäle.
Sie wusch die Gläser vom Absinth
Doch nie sich selber rein
Und doch muß die Hanna Cash, mein Kind
Auch rein gewesen sein.

3

Und sie kam eines Nachts in die Seemannsbar
Mit den Augen der schwarzen Seen
Und traf J. Kent mit dem Maulwurfshaar
Den Messerjack aus der Seemannsbar
Und der ließ sie mit sich gehn!
Und wenn der wüste Kent den Grind
Sich kratzte und blinzelte

BALLAD OF HANNAH CASH

1

With her plain print dress and her yellow shawl
And eyes like lakes as black as jet
No money and no talent and yet quite a lot
Of black hair which she wore hanging down
To her toes which were blacker yet.
And that was Hannah Cash, my child,
Who gypped her gentlemen so.
With the wind that blew across the savannas
She did come and go.

2

Her feet were bare. She'd no slip to wear
And she didn't know any hymn tunes.
Washed into the city like a little gray kitty
Wedged in among the gray driftwood
She was washed among the corpses to the black lagoons.
She washed the absinthe glasses, though
Herself she did not wash
And yet she must have been very clean
Must this Hannah Cash.

3

She came from afar to The Seaman's Bar.
It was there that she met J. Kent.
She had eyes like lakes, he had hair like a mole
And was Jack the Knife of The Seaman's Bar!
And off with him she went.
The brutish Kent had only to blink
And scratch his moleskin nut

Dann spürt die Hanna Cash, mein Kind
Den Blick bis in die Zeh.

4

Sie „kamen sich näher" zwischen Wild und Fisch
Und „gingen vereint durchs Leben"
Sie hatten kein Bett und sie hatten keinen Tisch
Und sie hatten selber nicht Wild noch Fisch
Und keinen Namen für die Kinder.
Doch ob Schneewind pfeift, ob Regen rinnt
Ersöff auch die Savann
Es bleibt die Hanna Cash, mein Kind
Bei ihrem lieben Mann.

5

Der Sheriff sagt, daß es 'n Schurke sei
Und die Milchfrau sagt: er geht krumm.
Sie aber sagt: Was ist dabei?
Es ist mein Mann. Und sie war so frei
Und blieb bei ihm. Darum.
Und wenn er hinkt und wenn er spinnt
Und wenn er ihr Schläge gibt:
Es fragt die Hanna Cash, mein Kind
Doch nur: ob sie ihn liebt.

6

Kein Dach war da, wo die Wiege war
Und die Schläge schlugen die Eltern.
Die gingen zusammen Jahr für Jahr
Aus der Asphaltstadt in die Wälder gar
Und in die Savann aus den Wäldern.
Solang man geht in Schnee und Wind
Bis daß man nicht mehr kann

And Hannah Cash would feel the blink
From her head to her black, black foot.

4
'Twixt the fish and the game they closer came.
One life the other joins.
They have no table and they have no bed
Nor fish nor game nor even a name
For the children of their loins.
Oh, the wind may blow, and there may be snow,
The savanna may be drowned in rain
But this Hannah Cash, my child,
With the man she loves will remain.

5
The milk girl declares he's a cripple.
The sheriff says he breaks the laws.
And what of that? Says she thereat.
He is my man. And she makes bold
To stay with him. Because.
Oh, he may be lame, and he may be insane,
He may beat her till she's yellow
But Hannah only asks herself
If she loves the fellow.

6
They fought all day where the cradle lay
With no roof to keep out the weather
From the city's asphalt scene to the forest green
And from the forests to the savannas
Year after year together!
How far can you go in the wind and the snow?
You can go as far as you can.

Solang ging die Hanna Cash, mein Kind
Nun mal mit ihrem Mann.

7

Kein Kleid war arm, wie das ihre war
Und es gab keinen Sonntag für sie
Keinen Ausflug zu dritt in die Kirschtortenbar
Und keinen Weizenfladen im Kar
Und keine Mundharmonie.
Und war jeder Tag, wie alle sind
Und gab's kein Sonnenlicht:
Es hatte die Hanna Cash, mein Kind,
Die Sonn stets im Gesicht.

8

Er stahl wohl die Fische, und Salz stahl sie
So war's. „Das Leben ist schwer."
Und wenn sie die Fische kochte, sieh:
So sagten die Kinder auf seinem Knie
Den Katechismus her.
Durch fünfzig Jahr in Nacht und Wind
Sie schliefen in einem Bett.
Das war die Hanna Cash, mein Kind
Gott mach's ihr einmal wett.

And that's how far this Hannah went
Alongside her man.

7

No dress is so poor as her dress is poor.
There are no Sundays for her
No rides on carts, no cakes or tarts
No restaurants with man and child
And no harmonica.
But though every day was like every day
And there was no sunlight
This Hannah Cash had the sun in her face
All day and all the night.

8

Yes, he stole the fish, and she stole salt.
Life is hard: that's a truism.
When she goes to cook, just take a look:
The children are sitting on his knee
Reciting their catechism!
Side by side they slept as the night winds wept
Fifty years and more.
And that was Hannah Cash. May God
Make it up to her!

ERINNERUNG AN DIE MARIE A.

1

An jenem Tag im blauen Mond September
Still unter einem jungen Pflaumenbaum
Da hielt ich sie, die stille bleiche Liebe
In meinem Arm wie einen holden Traum.
Und über uns im schönen Sommerhimmel
War eine Wolke, die ich lange sah
Sie war sehr weiß und ungeheuer oben
Und als ich aufsah, war sie nimmer da.

2

Seit jenem Tag sind viele, viele Monde
Geschwommen still hinunter und vorbei
Die Pflaumenbäume sind wohl abgehauen
Und fragst du mich, was mit der Liebe sei?
So sag ich dir: Ich kann mich nicht erinnern.
Und doch, gewiß, ich weiß schon, was du meinst
Doch ihr Gesicht, das weiß ich wirklich nimmer
Ich weiß nur mehr: Ich küßte es dereinst.

3

Und auch den Kuß, ich hätt' ihn längst vergessen
Wenn nicht die Wolke da gewesen wär
Die weiß ich noch und werd ich immer wissen
Sie war sehr weiß und kam von oben her.
Die Pflaumenbäume blühn vielleicht noch immer
Und jene Frau hat jetzt vielleicht das siebte Kind
Doch jene Wolke blühte nur Minuten
Und als ich aufsah, schwand sie schon im Wind.

MEMORY OF MARIE A.*

1

Upon that day, a day of blue September,
Silent and still beneath a young plum tree,
I held my silent, still, and pale belovèd,
And in my arms a golden dream was she.
And in the wide and lovely summer heavens
There was a cloud, and long I saw it there.
It was pure white and, oh, so high above us:
When I looked up, it vanished in the air.

2

And since that moment, many a September
Came sailing in, then floated down the stream.
No doubt the plum trees were cut down for timber
And if you ask what happened to my dream
I shall reply: I cannot now remember
Though what you have in mind I surely know.
And yet her face: I really don't recall it.
I just recall I kissed it long ago.

3

Even the kiss would have been long forgotten
If that white cloud had not been in the sky.
I know the cloud, and shall know it forever,
It was pure white and, oh, so very high.
Perhaps the plum trees still are there and blooming.
Perhaps that woman has six children too.
But that white cloud bloomed only for a moment:
When I looked up, it vanished in the blue.

---

*Copyright © 1963 by Eric Bentley.

BALLADE VOM MAZEPPA

1

Mit eigenem Strick verstrickt dem eigenen Pferde
Sie schnürten ihn Rücken an Rücken dem Roß
Das wild aufwiehernd über heimatliche Erde
Gehetzt in den dunkelnden Abend hinschoß.

2

Sie schnürten ihn so, daß den Gaul der Verstrickte
Im Schmerz noch aufpeitschte durch sinnloses Zerrn
Und so, daß er nichts, nur den Himmel erblickte
Der dunkler ward, weiter ward, ferner als fern.

3

Wohl trug ihn der Gaul vor der hetzenden Meute
Blind und verzweifelt und treu wie ein Weib
Ihm riß er, je mehr seine Feinde er scheute
Tiefer den Strick im blutwäßrigen Leib.

4

Auch füllte sich abends dann seltsam der Himmel
Mit fremdem Gevögel: Kräh und Geier, die mit
Lautlosem Flug in dunklem Gewimmel
Im Äther verfolgen den keuchenden Ritt.

5

Drei Tage trug ihn der fleischerne Teller
Wiehernd hinab an den ewigen Start
Wo der Himmel bald dunkler und wo er bald heller
Doch immer unermeßlicher ward.

BALLAD OF MAZEPPA

1

He was bound with a rope of his own to his horse, and
They fastened him back to back on the beast
Which whinnying wildly o'er the earth of his homeland
Shot off as if hunted in darkening night.

2

They fastened him so that he whipped the horse on
Chafing his back with a meaningless spur
And so he could see nothing else but the sky which
Grew darker and wider and farther than far.

3

Yes, the nag bore him far from the menacing many
Blind and despairing and true as a wife
And the farther he fled from his foes the deeper
The rope cut his body midst water and blood.

4

And strangely the sky filled up in the evening
With alien birds: the vulture and crow
Which with noiseless wings in the dusky tumult
Pursued through the ether the gasping ride.

5

Three days that plate of horseflesh bore him
Whinnying down to where all begins
Where the sky's now darker, now lighter, but ever
More and more immeasurable.

6

Drei Tage immer gehetzter und schneller
Drei Ewigkeiten lang war die Fahrt
Wo der Himmel dunkler und wo er bald heller
Doch immer unermeßlicher ward.

7

Drei Tage will er zum Sterben sich strecken
Er kann's nicht im Flug zwischen Himmel und Gras
Und die Geier lauern schon auf sein Verrecken
Und sehnen sich wild auf das lebende Aas.

8

Drei Tage, bis seine Stricke sich sträubten
Grün war der Himmel und braun war das Gras!
Ach! es rauften wohl immer zu seinen Häupten
Kräh und Geier sich schon um das lebende Aas!

9

Und ritt er schneller, sie folgten ihm gerne.
Und schrie er lauter, sie schrien mit
Beschattend die Sonn' und beschattend die Sterne
Verfolgten sie seinen keuchenden Ritt.

10

Drei Tage, dann mußte alles sich zeigen:
Erde gibt Schweigen und Himmel gibt Ruh.
Einer ritt aus mit dem, was ihm zu eigen:
Mit Erde und Pferd, mit Langmut und Schweigen
Dann kamen noch Himmel und Geier dazu.

6

Three days that were ever more haunted, more hunted,
Three eternities long was the ride
Where the sky's now darker, now lighter, but ever
More and more immeasurable.

7

For three days he wanted to stretch out and finish.
He cannot: in flight 'twixt the sky and the grass.
And the vultures keep watch for the hour of his dying
Mad with desire for the still living meat.

8

Three days! Till his ropes all stiffened and bristled
And green were the skies and brown was the grass!
Oh, the crow and the vulture already were brawling
High over his head for the still living meat!

9

And if he rode faster, they followed him gladly
And if he screamed louder, they screamed with him
And throwing the sun and the stars into shadow
They went on pursuing his gasping ride.

10

Three days! Till things reached their conclusion.
For earth gives silence, the heavens give sleep.
One man rode out with whate'er was vouchsafed him:
The earth and a horse and endurance and silence.
And the heavens and the vultures were added thereto.

11

Drei Tage lang ritt er durch Abend und Morgen
Bis er alt genug war, daß er nicht mehr litt
Als er gerettet ins große Geborgen
Todmüd in die ewige Ruhe einritt.

11

For three days he rode through the night and the day till
He was old enough not to suffer when he
In the final haven met his salvation
And, weary, rode into perpetual peace.

BALLADE VON DER FREUNDSCHAFT

1

Wie zwei Kürbisse abwärts schwimmen
Verfault, doch an einem Stiel
In gelben Flüssen: Sie trieben
Mit Karten und Worten ihr Spiel.
Und sie schossen nach den gelben Monden
Und sie liebten sich und sahn nicht hin:
Blieben sie vereint in vielen Nächten
Und auch: wenn die Sonne schien.

2

In den grünen harten Gesträuchern
Wenn der Himmel bewölkt war, der Hund,
Sie hingen wie ranzige Datteln
Einander sanft in den Mund.
Und auch später, wenn die Zähne ihnen
Aus den Kiefern fieln, sie sahen nicht hin:
Blieben doch vereint in vielen Nächten
Und auch: wenn die Sonne schien.

3

In den kleinen räudigen Häusern
Befriedigten sie ihren Leib
Und im Dschungel, wenn daran Not war
Hinterm Strauch bei dem gleichen Weib.
Doch am Morgen wuschen sie die Hemden
Gingen Arm in Arm fort, Knie an Knien
Vereint sie in vielen Nächten
Und auch: wenn die Sonne schien.

BALLAD OF FRIENDSHIP

1

As when two pumpkins swim downstream
In yellow rivers, on one stalk,
And rotten: so these two men played
Their game of playing-cards and words.
They took potshots at the yellow moons
And they made love and did not look.
They were together many nights
And also when the sun was shining.

2

And when that S.O.B. the sky
Was overcast, those two lay down
In hard green shrubbery and dangling
Like rancid dates in each other's mouths.
And later, too, when all their teeth
Fell from their jaws, they did not look.
They were together many nights
And also when the sun was shining.

3

In mangy little outhouses
They satisfied their bodies' need
Or in the jungle's undergrowth
—If need be, with the same female.
When morning came, they'd wash their shirts
And leave, arm in arm, knee to knee.
They were together many nights
And also when the sun was shining.

4

Als es kälter auf Erden wurde
Dach fehlte und Zeitvertreib
Unter anderen Schlingpflanzen lagen
Umschlungen sie da, Leib an Leib.
Wenn sie reden in den Sternennächten
Hören sie mitunter nicht mehr hin:
Vereint sie in vielen Nächten
Und auch: wenn die Sonne schien.

5

Aber einmal kam jene Insel
Manchen Mond wohnten beide sie dort
Und als sie fort wollten beide
Konnte einer nimmer mit fort.
Und sie sahn nach Wind und Flut und Schiffen
Aber niemals nach dem andern hin
Vereint sie, in vielen Nächten
Und auch: wenn die Sonne schien.

6

„Fahr du, Kamerad, denn ich kann nicht.
Mich frißt die Salzflut entzwei
Hier kann ich noch etwas liegen
Eine Woche noch oder zwei."
Und ein Mann liegt krank am Wasser
Und blickt stumm zu einem Manne hin
Der ihm einst vereint, in vielen Nächten
Und auch: wenn die Sonne schien.

7

„Ich liege hier gut! Fahr zu, Kamerad!"
„Laß es sein, Kamerad, es hat Zeit!"

4

When it got colder on the earth
And they'd no roof or aught to do
Under other creeping plants they'd lie
Body by body and embracing.
And when they talked in the starry night
They were not always listening.
They were together many nights
And also when the sun was shining.

5

And then one time an island came
Whereon they stayed for many a moon
And when they both desired to leave
One of them was not able to.
They kept a lookout for wind and ships.
In each other's eyes they did not look.
They were together many nights
And also when the sun was shining.

6

"You go, my friend, for I cannot.
The salt flood's rotting my insides.
I can stay here a little while,
One week perhaps, or maybe two."
And by the water a man lies sick
And dumbly gazes at a man
Who had been with him many nights
And also when the sun was shining.

7

"I'm all right lying here: you go!"
"Let be, my friend, let be: there's time."

„Wenn der Regen kommt und du bist nicht fort
Faulen wir schwarz zu zweit!"
Und ein Hemd weht, und im Salzwind steht ein
Mann und blickt aufs Wasser hin und ihn
Der ihm einst vereint in so vielen Nächten
Und auch: wenn die Sonne schien.

8

Und jetzt kam der Tag, wo sie schieden!
Die Dattel spuck aus, die verdorrt!
Oft sahen sie nachts nach dem Winde
Und am Morgen ging einer fort.
Gingen noch zu zweit in frischen Hemden
Arm in Arm und rauchend, Knie an Knien
Vereint sie, in vielen Nächten
Und auch: wenn die Sonne schien.

9

„Kamerad, der Wind geht ins Segel!"
„Der Wind geht bis morgen früh!"
„Kamerad, ich bitte dich, binde
Mir dort an den Baum meine Knie!"
Und der andre Mann band rauchend fest ihn
Mit dem Strick an jenem Baume ihn
Der ihm einst vereint in vielen Nächten
Und auch: wenn die Sonne schien.

10

„Kamerad, vor dem Mond sind schon Wolken!"
„Der Wind treibt sie weg, es hat Zeit."
„Kamerad, ich sehe dir nach noch:
Von dem Baum aus sieht man weit."
Und nach Tagen, als der Strick durchbissen

"If rain should come and you still here
We'd rot and then turn black together."
A shirt waves in the wind. A man
Gazes at the water and at him
Who had been with him many nights
And also when the sun was shining.

8

The day arrived for them to part.
Spit out the dried-up date, don't eat it!
At night they looked how the wind was blowing:
For in the morning one would leave.
They walked together in clean shirts
Arm in arm, and smoking, knee to knee.
They were together many nights
And also when the sun was shining.

9

"My friend, the wind has caught the sail."
"The wind will blow till tomorrow morning."
"Take a rope, my friend, and tie my knees
To the tree—that tree over there."
The other, smoking, took a rope
And to the tree there tied him down
Who had been with him many nights
And also when the sun was shining.

10

"The moon is covered with clouds, my friend."
"The wind will drive them off: there's time."
"From this tree one can see very far:
I'll follow you with my eyes, my friend."
Days passed, the rope was bitten through,

Schaut er immer noch aufs Wasser hin
In den wenigen und letzten Nächten
Und auch: wenn die Sonne schien.

11

Aber jener, in vielen Wochen
Auf dem Meer, bei der Frau, im Gesträuch:
Es verblassen viele Himmel
Doch der Mann am Baum wird nicht bleich:
Die Gespräche in den Sternennächten
Arm in Arm und rauchend, Knie an Knien
Die sie stets vereint, in vielen Nächten
Und auch: wenn die Sonne schien.

And he was watching the water still
In the last nights, which were not many,
And also when the sun was shining.

11

That fellow, though, in many weeks
On sea, with women, in undergrowth,
Though many skies turn pale, the man
Beside the tree fades not at all
Nor do the talks on starry nights
Arm in arm, and, smoking, knee to knee
Which kept them together many nights
And also when the sun was shining.

DIE BALLADE VON DEM SOLDATEN

1

Das Schießgewehr schießt und das Spießmesser spießt
Und das Wasser frißt auf, die drin waten.
Was könnt ihr gegen Eis? Bleibt weg, 's ist nicht weis'!
Sagte das Weib zum Soldaten.

2

Doch der Soldat mit der Kugel im Lauf
Hörte die Trommel und lachte darauf
Marschieren kann nimmermehr schaden!
Hinab nach dem Süden, nach dem Norden hinauf
Und das Messer fängt er mit Händen auf!
Sagten zum Weib die Soldaten.

3

Ach, bitter bereut, wer des Weisen Rat scheut
Und vom Alter sich nicht läßt beraten!
Ach, zu hoch nicht hinaus, es geht übel aus!
Sagte das Weib zum Soldaten.

4

Doch der Soldat mit dem Messer im Gurt
Lacht ihr kalt ins Gesicht und ging über die Furt
Was konnte das Wasser ihm schaden?
Wenn weiß der Mond überm Mongefluß steht
Kommen wir wieder; nimm's auf ins Gebet!
Sagten zum Weib die Soldaten.

THE BALLAD OF THE SOLDIER

1

Oh, a gun will gun, and a lance will lance,
And the water will swallow those who wade in it!
How can *you* fight the ice? Keep away, it's unwise!
Said the woman to the soldier.

2

The soldier, though, with a bullet in his gun,
Heard the drum roll and laughed at the fun:
Marching could never hurt him!
In the southern and in the northern lands
He parries the lance with his naked hands!
Said the soldiers to the woman.

3

Woe to him who defies the advice of the wise
And will not be guided by his elders!
Don't you aim too high or you'll end in the sky!
Said the woman to the soldier.

4

The soldier, though, he took up his sword,
Laughed coldly in her face and entered the ford:
How could the water hurt him?
And when on the Monge the moon shines white
We are all coming back: go pray for that night!
Said the soldiers to the woman.

5

Ihr vergeht wie der Rauch, und die Wärme geht auch
Und uns wärmen nicht eure Taten!
Ach, wie schnell geht der Rauch! Gott, behüte ihn auch!
Sagte das Weib vom Soldaten.

6

Und der Soldat mit dem Messer am Gurt
Sank hin mit dem Speer, und mit riß ihn die Furt
Und das Wasser fraß auf, die drin waten.
Kühl stand der Mond überm Mongefluß weiß
Doch der Soldat trieb hinab mit dem Eis
Und was sagten dem Weib die Soldaten?

7

Er verging wie der Rauch, und die Wärme ging auch
Und es wärmten sie nicht seine Taten.
Ach bitter bereut, wer des Weibes Rat scheut!
Sagte das Weib zum Soldaten.

5

Like smoke you'll pass on! The warm air will be gone!
And your great deeds will not warm us!
How fast the smoke goes! God save *him* from his foes!
Said the woman of the soldier.

6

The soldier, though, with his gun and his sword,
Sank with his spear in the clutch of the ford:
And the water swallowed those who waded in it.
Cool above the Monge the moon shone white
But the soldier floated along with the ice.
And what did the soldiers tell the woman?

7

Like smoke he passed on and the warm air was gone
And his great deeds did not warm them.
Woe to him who defies the woman's advice!
Said the woman to the soldier.

VIERTE LEKTION

Mahagonnygesänge

FOURTH LESSON

Mahagonny Songs

AUF NACH MAHAGONNY!

1

Auf nach Mahagonny
Die Luft ist kühl und frisch
Dort gibt es Pferd- und Weiberfleisch
Whisky- und Pokertisch.
     Schöner grüner Mond von Mahagonny, leuchte uns!
     Denn wir haben heute hier
     Unterm Hemde Geldpapier
     Für ein großes Lachen deines großen dummen Munds.

2

Auf nach Mahagonny
Der Ostwind, der geht schon
Dort gibt es frischen Fleischsalat
Und keine Direktion.
     Schöner grüner Mond von Mahagonny, leuchte uns!
     Denn wir haben heute hier
     Unterm Hemde Geldpapier
     Für ein großes Lachen deines großen dummen Munds.

3

Auf nach Mahagonny
Das Schiff wird losgeseilt
Die Zi-zi-zi-zi-zivilis,
Die wird uns dort geheilt.
     Schöner grüner Mond von Mahagonny, leuchte uns!
     Denn wir haben heute hier
     Unterm Hemde Geldpapier
     Für ein großes Lachen deines großen dummen Munds.

OFF TO MAHAGONNY!

1

Off to Mahagonny!
The air is fresh and cool
There's horse meat there and woman meat
And whisky, cards, and pool.

     Beautiful green moon of Mahagonny, shine on us!
     For beneath our shirts today
     We have dough with which to pay
     For a great big laugh upon your great big stupid puss!

2

Off to Mahagonny!
An East wind is on hand
The salad there's made of fresh meat
And no one's in command.

     Beautiful green moon of Mahagonny, shine on us!
     For beneath our shirts today
     We have dough with which to pay
     For a great big laugh upon your great big stupid puss!

3

Off to Mahagonny!
Our good ship is unmoored
And there our ci-ci-civiliz-
ation will soon be cured.

     Beautiful green moon of Mahagonny, shine on us!
     For beneath our shirts today
     We have dough with which to pay
     For a great big laugh upon your great big stupid puss!

WER IN MAHAGONNY BLIEB

Wer in Mahagonny blieb
Brauchte jeden Tag fünf Dollar
Und wenn er's besonders trieb
Brauchte er vielleicht noch extra.
Aber damals blieben alle
In Mahagonnys Pokerdrinksaloon
Sie verloren in jedem Falle
Doch sie hatten was davon.

1

Auf der See und am Land
Werden allen Leuten ihre Häute abgezogen
Darum sitzen alle Leute
Und verkaufen alle Häute
Denn die Häute werden jederzeit mit Dollars
            aufgewogen.
            Wer in Mahagonny blieb
            Brauchte jeden Tag fünf Dollar
            Und wenn er's besonders trieb
            Brauchte er vielleicht noch extra.
            Aber damals blieben alle
            In Mahagonnys Pokerdrinksaloon
            Sie verloren in jedem Falle
            Doch sie hatten was davon.

2

Auf der See und am Land
Ist drum der Verbrauch von frischen Häuten ungeheuer
Immer beißt es euch im Fleische
Doch wer zahlt euch eure Räusche?

TO STAY IN MAHAGONNY, YOU

To stay in Mahagonny, you
Need about five bucks per diem.
And if you work hard then you
Need perhaps a wee bit extra.
They all were staying at the time
In Mahagonny's poker-drink-saloon.
And they lost in any case but
They got something out of it.

1

On the sea and on land
Absolutely everybody's skin is taken off him.
Everybody sits and sells the
Skin off every other body.
Skin's a thing that at all times can be converted into dollars.
>   *To stay in Mahagonny, you*
>   *Need about five bucks per diem.*
>   *And if you work hard then you*
>   *Need perhaps a wee bit extra.*
>   *They all were staying at the time*
>   *In Mahagonny's poker-drink-saloon.*
>   *And they lost in any case but*
>   *They got something out of it.*

2

On the sea and on land
The consumption of fresh skins is becoming quite a business.
No question, it gives you a thrill, sir.
The question is who pays the bill, sir.

Denn die Häute, die sind billig, und der Whisky,
                    der ist teuer.
Wer in Mahagonny blieb
Brauchte jeden Tag fünf Dollar
Und wenn er's besonders trieb
Brauchte er vielleicht noch extra.
Aber damals blieben alle
In Mahagonnys Pokerdrinksaloon
Sie verloren in jedem Falle
Doch sie hatten was davon.

3

Auf der See und am Land
Siehet man die vielen Gottesmühlen langsam mahlen
Und drum sitzen viele Leute
Und verkaufen viele Häute
Denn sie wolln so gern bar leben und so
                    ungern bar bezahlen.
Wer in seinem Kober bleibt
Braucht nicht jeden Tag fünf Dollar
Und falls er nicht unbeweibt
Braucht er auch vielleicht nicht extra.
Aber heute sitzen alle
In des lieben Gottes billigem Salon
Sie gewinnen in jedem Falle
Und sie haben nichts davon.

Though the skins are inexpensive whisky can run into money.

> *To stay in Mahagonny, you*
> *Need about five bucks per diem.*
> *And if you work hard then you*
> *Need perhaps a wee bit extra.*
> *They all were staying at the time*
> *In Mahagonny's poker-drink-saloon.*
> *And they lost in any case but*
> *They got something out of it.*

3

On the sea and on land
One sees the many mills of God Almighty grinding slowly.
That's why many people sit here
Selling many people's skin here.
For they like to call the tune but do not like to pay the piper.

> *If you stay at home then you*
> *Do not need five bucks per diem.*
> *And if you are married, you*
> *Do not need that wee bit extra.*
> *But they all have come to stay*
> *In God Almighty's second-class saloon.*
> *And they win in any case but*
> *They get nothing out of it.*

GOTT IN MAHAGONNY

An einem grauen Vormittag
Mitten im Whisky
Kam Gott nach Mahagonny
Kam Gott nach Mahagonny.
Mitten im Whisky
Bemerkten wir Gott in Mahagonny.

1

Sauft ihr wie die Schwämme
Meinen guten Weizen Jahr für Jahr?
Keiner hat erwartet, daß ich käme
Wenn ich komme jetzt, ist alles gar?
Ansahen sich die Männer von Mahagonny.
Ja, sagten die Männer von Mahagonny.

An einem grauen Vormittag
Mitten im Whisky
Kam Gott nach Mahagonny
Kam Gott nach Mahagonny.
Mitten im Whisky
Bemerkten wir Gott in Mahagonny.

2

Lachtet ihr am Freitag abend?
Mary Weemann sah ich ganz von fern
Wie 'nen Stockfisch stumm im Salzsee schwimmen
Sie wird nicht mehr trocken, meine Herrn.
Ansahen sich die Männer von Mahagonny.
Ja, sagten die Männer von Mahagonny.

An einem grauen Vormittag
Mitten im Whisky
Kam Gott nach Mahagonny

GOD IN MAHAGONNY

On a gray morning
All among the whisky
God came to Mahagonny
God came to Mahagonny.
All among the whisky
We noticed God had come to Mahagonny.

1

As sponges suck up water
Do you devour my grain from year to year?
None of you believed that I was coming.
When I do come, is the cupboard bare?
All the men of Mahagonny looked at one another.
Yes, said the men of Mahagonny.
> *On a gray morning*
> *All among the whisky*
> *God came to Mahagonny*
> *God came to Mahagonny.*
> *All among the whisky*
> *We noticed God had come to Mahagonny.*

2

Were you laughing Friday evening?
Mary Weemann from afar I could descry
Swimming like a codfish in the salt lake:
Gentlemen, she never will be dry.
All the men of Mahagonny looked at one another.
True, said the men of Mahagonny.
> *On a gray morning*
> *All among the whisky*
> *God came to Mahagonny*

Kam Gott nach Mahagonny.
Mitten im Whisky
Bemerkten wir Gott in Mahagonny.

3

Kennt ihr diese Patronen?
Schießt ihr meinen guten Missionar?
Soll ich wohl mit euch im Himmel wohnen
Sehen euer graues Säuferhaar?
Ansahen sich die Männer von Mahagonny.
Ja, sagten die Männer von Mahagonny.
> *An einem grauen Vormittag*
> *Mitten im Whisky*
> *Kam Gott nach Mahagonny*
> *Kam Gott nach Mahagonny.*
> *Mitten im Whisky*
> *Bemerkten wir Gott in Mahagonny.*

4

Gehet alle zur Hölle
Steckt jetzt die Virginien in den Sack!
Marsch mit euch in meine Hölle, Burschen
In die schwarze Hölle mit euch Pack!
Ansahen sich die Männer von Mahagonny.
Ja, sagten die Männer von Mahagonny.
> *An einem grauen Vormittag*
> *Mitten im Whisky*
> *Kommst du nach Mahagonny*
> *Kommst du nach Mahagonny.*
> *Mitten im Whisky*
> *Fängst an du in Mahagonny!*

God came to Mahagonny.
All among the whisky
We noticed God had come to Mahagonny.

3

Do you recognize these bullets?
Did you shoot my missionary dead?
D'you think I'd want to live with you in Heaven
And gaze upon your graying drunkards' heads?
All the men of Mahagonny looked at one another.
Yes, said the men of Mahagonny.

On a gray morning
All among the whisky
God came to Mahagonny
God came to Mahagonny.
All among the whisky
We noticed God had come to Mahagonny.

4

Hell's the place for you then!
So put your cigars away and pack!
Off to hell with all of you rapscallions!
Go to hell, my lads, where it is black!
All the men of Mahagonny looked at one another.
Yes, said the men of Mahagonny.

On a gray morning
All among the whisky
You come to Mahagonny
You come to Mahagonny.
All among the whisky
You cut loose in Mahagonny!

5

Rühre keiner den Fuß jetzt!
Jedermann streikt! An den Haaren
Kannst du uns nicht in die Hölle ziehen:
Weil wir immer in der Hölle waren.
Ansahen Gott die Männer von Mahagonny.
Nein, sagten die Männer von Mahagonny.

5

No one make a move now!
We're all on strike! And you can't very well, sir,
Send us to hell, not if you drag us by the hair:
Because we always were in hell, sir.
They looked at God, did the men of Mahagonny.
No, said the men of Mahagonny.

ALABAMA SONG
(Written in English by Bertolt Brecht)

1

Oh, show us the way to the next whisky-bar
Oh, don't ask why, oh, don't ask why
For we must find the next whisky-bar
For if we don't find the next whisky-bar
I tell you we must die! I tell you we must die!
Oh! Moon of Alabama
We now must say good-bye
We've lost our good old mamma
And must have whisky
Oh! You know why.

2

Oh, show us the way to the next pretty girl
Oh, don't ask why, oh, don't ask why
For we must find the next pretty girl
For if we don't find the next pretty girl
I tell you we must die! I tell you we must die!
Oh! Moon of Alabama
We now must say good-bye
We've lost our good old mamma
And must have a girl
Oh! You know why.

3

Oh, show us the way to the next little dollar
Oh, don't ask why, oh, don't ask why
For we must find the next little dollar
For if we don't find the next little dollar
I tell you we must die! I tell you we must die!

ALABAMA SONG
(*Written in English by Bertolt Brecht*)

1

Oh, show us the way to the next whisky-bar
Oh, don't ask why, oh, don't ask why
For we must find the next whisky-bar
For if we don't find the next whisky-bar
I tell you we must die! I tell you we must die!
> *Oh! Moon of Alabama*
> *We now must say good-bye*
> *We've lost our good old mamma*
> *And must have whisky*
> *Oh! You know why.*

2

Oh, show us the way to the next pretty girl
Oh, don't ask why, oh, don't ask why
For we must find the next pretty girl
For if we don't find the next pretty girl
I tell you we must die! I tell you we must die!
> *Oh! Moon of Alabama*
> *We now must say good-bye*
> *We've lost our good old mamma*
> *And must have a girl*
> *Oh! You know why.*

3

Oh, show us the way to the next little dollar
Oh, don't ask why, oh, don't ask why
For we must find the next little dollar
For if we don't find the next little dollar
I tell you we must die! I tell you we must die!

Oh! Moon of Alabama
We now must say good-bye
We've lost our good old mamma
And must have dollars
Oh! You know why.

Oh! Moon of Alabama
We now must say good-bye
We've lost our good old mamma
And must have dollars
Oh! You know why.

BENARES SONG
(*Written in English by Bertolt Brecht*)

1

There is no whisky in this town
There is no bar to sit us down
Oh!
Where is the telephone?
Is here no telephone?
Oh, Sir, God damn me:
No!

> *Let's go to Benares*
> *Where the sun is shining*
> *Let's go to Benares!*
> *Johnny, let us go.*

2

There is no money in this land
There is no girl with whom to shake hands
Oh!
Where is the telephone?
Is here no telephone?
Oh, Sir, God damn me:
No!

> *Let's go to Benares*
> *Where the sun is shining*
> *Let's go to Benares!*
> *Johnny, let us go.*

3

There is not much fun on this star
There is no door that is ajar
Oh!

BENARES SONG
(Written in English by Bertolt Brecht)

1

There is no whisky in this town
There is no bar to sit us down
Oh!
Where is the telephone?
Is here no telephone?
Oh, Sir, God damn me:
No!

> *Let's go to Benares*
> *Where the sun is shining*
> *Let's go to Benares!*
> *Johnny, let us go.*

2

There is no money in this land
There is no girl with whom to shake hands
Oh!
Where is the telephone?
Is here no telephone?
Oh, Sir, God damn me:
No!

> *Let's go to Benares*
> *Where the sun is shining*
> *Let's go to Benares!*
> *Johnny, let us go.*

3

There is not much fun on this star
There is no door that is ajar
Oh!

Where is the telephone?
Is here no telephone?
Oh, Sir, God damn me:
No!

> *Worst of all, Benares*
> *Is said to have perished in an earthquake!*
> *Oh! our good Benares!*
> *Oh, where shall we go!*
> *Worst of all, Benares*
> *Is said to have been punished in an earthquake!*
> *Oh! our good Benares!*
> *Oh! where shall we go!*

Where is the telephone?
Is here no telephone?
Oh, Sir, God damn me:
No!

> *Worst of all, Benares*
> *Is said to have perished in an earthquake!*
> *Oh! our good Benares!*
> *Oh, where shall we go!*
> *Worst of all, Benares*
> *Is said to have been punished in an earthquake!*
> *Oh! our good Benares!*
> *Oh! where shall we go!*

FÜNFTE LEKTION

Die kleinen Tagzeiten der Abgestorbenen

FIFTH LESSON

The Little Hours of the Dead

CHORAL VOM MANNE BAAL

1

Als im weißen Mutterschoße aufwuchs Baal
War der Himmel schon so groß und still und fahl
Jung und nackt und ungeheuer wundersam
Wie ihn Baal dann liebte, als Baal kam.

2

Und der Himmel blieb in Lust und Kummer da
Auch wenn Baal schlief, selig war und ihn nicht sah:
Nachts er violett und trunken Baal
Baal früh fromm, er aprikosenfahl.

3

In der Sünder schamvollem Gewimmel
Lag Baal nackt und wälzte sich voll Ruh:
Nur der Himmel, aber *immer* Himmel
Deckte mächtig seine Blöße zu.

4

Alle Laster sind zu etwas gut
Und der Mann auch, sagt Baal, der sie tut.
Laster sind was, weiß man was man will.
Sucht euch zwei aus: eines ist zuviel!

5

Seid nur nicht so faul und so verweicht
Denn Genießen ist bei Gott nicht leicht!
Starke Glieder braucht man und Erfahrung auch:
Und mitunter stört ein dicker Bauch.

CHORALE OF THE MAN BAAL*

1

When inside the white maternal womb grew Baal
Large already was the sky and still and pale
Young and naked and almost miraculous
As Baal loved it when Baal came to us.

2

And the sky stayed there in woe or glee
Even when Baal slept in bliss and did not see.
Nights, the sky was mauve; Baal drank a lot.
Mornings, Baal was good; sky, pale as apricot.

3

And where shameless sinners rolled in lawlessness
Nonchalantly wallowing Baal lay.
Naught but sky to hide his nakedness
(Hide it, though, all day and every day)!

4

Every vice, says Baal, is good for something.
And so are the men who keep them going.
Vices can be worth a pretty penny.
Choose a couple, though! One is too many.

5

Do not be so lazy and so soft, do not!
To enjoy oneself, says Baal, is hard, by God!
And you need strong limbs. Experience, too, they say.
And a belly can be in the way.

6

Zu den feisten Geiern blinzelt Baal hinauf
Die im Sternenhimmel warten auf den Leichnam Baal
Manchmal stellt sich Baal tot. Stürzt ein Geier drauf
Speist Baal einen Geier, stumm, zum Abendmahl.

7

Unter düstern Sternen in dem Jammertal
Grast Baal weite Felder schmatzend ab.
Sind sie leer, dann trottet singend Baal
In den ewigen Wald zum Schlaf hinab.

8

Und wenn Baal der dunkle Schoß hinunterzieht:
Was ist Welt für Baal noch? Baal ist satt.
Soviel Himmel hat Baal unterm Lid
Daß er tot noch grad gnug Himmel hat.

9

Als im dunklen Erdenschoße faulte Baal
War der Himmel noch so groß und still und fahl
Jung und nackt und ungeheuer wunderbar
Wie ihn Baal einst liebte, als Baal war.

6

Baal, he blinks at well-fed vultures overhead
Waiting up among the stars till Baal is dead.
Often Baal shams dead. So if the bird
Falls for this, Baal dines on vulture, without a word.

7

In this vale of tears, and under gloomy stars,
Baal eats all the grass and smacks his lips.
When the fields are bare, Baal, singing, fares
To the everlasting forests where he sleeps.

8

When the dark womb drags Baal downward, O
What's the world to him? He's glad to go.
And beneath those eyelids Baal has sky to spare:
How could he use more now he lies there?

9

When inside the earth's dark belly rotted Baal
Large as ever was the sky and still and pale
Young and naked and almost miraculous
As Baal used to love it when Baal was.

VON DEN VERFÜHRTEN MÄDCHEN

1

Zu den seichten, braunversumpften Teichen
Wenn ich alt bin, führt mich der Teufel hinab.
Und er zeigt mir die Reste der Wasserleichen
Die ich auf meinem Gewissen hab.

2

Unter sehr getrübten Himmeln schwammen
Lässig und müde sie in die Hölle hinein
Wie ein Geflechte von Algen, alle zusammen
Wollen dort auf meine Kosten sein.

3

Ihre faulen entzündeten Leiber gaben
Einst mir Glut, die ich selber mir angefacht
Die den orangenen Tag mit mir genossen haben
Sie entzogen sich der düsteren Nacht.

4

Satt und bequem, als die schöne Speisung vorüber
Stießen aus Faulheit sie mich in Gewissensqual
Versauten die Erde mir, machten den Himmel mir trüber
Ließen mir einen entzündeten Leib und kein Bacchanal.

ON THE SEDUCED GIRLS

1

When I'm old the Devil comes and takes me
To the shallow, marshy ponds and brown
Shows me the remains of drowned cadavers
Which upon my guilty soul weigh down.

2

They had swum to hades, tired and lazy,
Under heavens gloomy and immense.
Stuck together like a web of algae
They'd like to stay there now at my expense.

3

Their inflamed and rotting bodies added
Fuel to the fire I had inside.
They enjoyed with me the orange daytime
Then from dusky night they crept and died.

4

When the lovely meal was done, replete and cozy
In their rottenness they made my conscience torture me,
Mucked up this earth for me, made the heavens still gloomier,
Left me a body inflamed and no bacchanalian spree.

VOM ERTRUNKENEN MÄDCHEN

1

Als sie ertrunken war und hinunterschwamm
Von den Bächen in die größeren Flüsse
Schien der Opal des Himmels sehr wundersam
Als ob er die Leiche begütigen müsse.

2

Tang und Algen hielten sich an ihr ein
So daß sie langsam viel schwerer ward
Kühl die Fische schwammen an ihrem Bein
Pflanzen und Tiere beschwerten noch ihre letzte Fahrt.

3

Und der Himmel ward abends dunkel wie Rauch
Und hielt nachts mit den Sternen das Licht in Schwebe.
Aber früh war er hell, daß es auch
Noch für sie Morgen und Abend gebe.

4

Als ihr bleicher Leib im Wasser verfaulet war,
Geschah es (sehr langsam), daß Gott sie allmählich vergaß
Erst ihr Gesicht, dann die Hände und ganz zuletzt
        erst ihr Haar.
Dann ward sie Aas in Flüssen mit vielem Aas.

ON THE DROWNED GIRL*

1

And when she had drowned and floated down
From rivulets and into larger rivers
The opal heavens shone most marvelously
As though they must propitiate the body.

2

Seaweed and algae, both held on to her,
And she slowly grew much heavier.
Fish coolly brushed against her leg.
Animals and plants weighed down her final voyage.

3

And the evening sky grew dark as smoke
And held, when evening passed, the light suspended.
In the morning, brightness came again:
There was night and morning even for her.

4

When her pale corpse rotted in the water
Very slowly God forgot her bit by bit:
First her face; her hands then; then last of all her hair.
In carrion-carrying rivers she was carrion.

DIE BALLADE VOM LIEBESTOD

1

Von schwarzem Regen siebenfach zerfressen
Ein schmieriger Gaumen, der die Liebe frißt
Mit Mullstors, die wie Totenlaken nässen:
Das ist die Kammer, die die letzte ist.

2

Aussätzig die Tapeten, weiß vom Schimmel!
In Hölzer sie gepfercht, verschweißt und hart:
Wie lieblich scheinet der verschlissne Himmel
Dem weißen Paare, das sich himmlisch paart.

3

Im Anfang sitzt er oft in nassen Tüchern
Und lutscht Virginias, schwarz, die sie ihm gibt
Und nützt die Zeit, ihr nickend zu versichern
Mit halbgeschlossenem Lid, daß er sie liebt.

4

Sie fühlt, wie er behaart ist und so weise!
Er sieht im Schlitz des Lids den Tag verschwemmt
Und grün wie Seife wölkt sich das Gehäuse
Des Himmels und ihm schwant: jetzt fault mein Hemd.

5

Sie gießen Kognak in die trocknen Leichen
Er füttert sie mit grünem Abendlicht
Und es entzünden sich schon ihre Weichen
Und es verblaßt schon mählich ihr Gesicht.

THE BALLAD OF THE LOVE-DEATH

Rotted by the black rain seven times over,
A filthy set of gums that feeds on love,
With muslin curtains that are damp as shrouds,
This is the bedroom. This is the last bedroom.
Leprous the wallpaper! White with mold!
And they are hard and sweaty and hemmed in.
How comely seem the seedy heavens to the white
Couple whose coupling is so heavenly!
At first he often sits there in damp cloths
And sucks cigars, the black ones that she gives him,
Using the time to assure her with a nod
And half-closed eyelid that he loves her.
How hairy he is, she feels. How wise as well!
Through his eyelid's slit the day is moist and bloated.
The sky's great building forms an arch as green
As soap. It dawns on him: My shirt's decaying.
And they pour cognac into their dry corpses.
He feeds her with the evening's green light.
And now their loins become inflamed again
And gradually their faces fade away.
She's like a meadow half submerged in water
(Orphans both, and deaf, and dull of flesh!).
He'd like to sleep if only she would let him!
A green sky he, that rained and finished raining!
On the second day they hide their corpses in
Stiff cloths and in the sweaty curtain, and
Cover their loins with filthy sheets because
They know now that they often had been freezing.
And, Oh! love went right through them like a knife!
As if through water God had hurled his hailstones!
And deep inside, eviscerating them,
There bubbled, thick as yeast, green bitterness.
With the stench of sweat and urine in their hair

6

Sie ist wie eine halbersoffne Wiese
[Sie sind verwaist und taub, im Fleische matt!]
Er will gern schlafen, wenn sie ihn nur ließe!
Ein grüner Himmel, der geregnet hat!

7

Am zweiten Tage hüllen sie die Leichen
In steife Tücher, den verschweißten Stor
Und nehmen schmierige Laken in die Weichen
Weil sie jetzt wissen, daß es sie oft fror.

8

Und ach, die Liebe ging durch sie so schneidend
Wie wenn Gott Hageleis durch Wasser schmiß!
Und tief in ihnen quoll, sie ganz ausweidend
Und dick wie Hefe grüne Bitternis.

9

Von Schweiß, Urin, Geruch in ihren Haaren
Sie wittern ferner nicht mehr Morgenluft.
Es kommt der Morgen wahrlich noch nach Jahren
Vertiert und grau in die Tapetengruft.

10

Ach, ihr zarter Kinderleib perlmuttern!
Holz und Liebe schlugen ihn so rauh
Schmilzt wie Holz salzflutzerschlagner Kutter
Unter Sturmflut! Gras in zuviel Tau!

They cannot smell the morning air any more.
And morning really comes, though after years,
Beastly and gray, to the wallpaper grave.
Her childlike body, tender, mother of pearl!
Bedboards and love have smitten it so roughly
It melts like planks of cutters felled by a storm
At sea! Grass plunged into too much dew!
And oh, the hand upon her breast—like grass!
A black stench of disease in both her legs!
On windowpanes the mild air floated off
And there they lay: in the decaying closet.
Evening floats like dishwater to the panes
And to the curtains scurvy with tobacco.
A pair of lovers is sailing in green waters
Soaked through with rain of love, like some old wreck
On the sea's bottom in the tropics, which,
Burst open, hangs between whitish fish and algae,
And, from the salt wind blowing on the surface,
In the waters underneath begins to rock.
On the fourth day, very early on, with strokes
Of grating axes neighbors broke in.
They heard the stillness and they saw the bodies.
They muttered about a greenish shimmer that faces
Can give off. The bed still reeked of love.
Frost burst the window. Corpses are cold things! Look,
A black thread of cold was crawling from their breasts!

11
Ach, die Hand an ihrer Brust wie gräsern!
In den Beinen schwarzer Pestgestank!
Milde Luft floß ab an Fenstergläsern
Und sie staken im verfaulten Schrank!

12
Wie Spülicht floß der Abend an die Scheiben
Und die Gardinen räudig von Tabak.
In grünen Wassern zwei Geliebte treiben
Von Liebe ganz durchregnet, wie ein Wrack

13
Am Meergrund, das, geborsten, in den Tropen
Zwischen Algen und weißlichen Fischen hängt
Und von einem Salzwind über der Fläche oben
Tief in den Wassern unten zu schaukeln anfängt.

14
Am vierten Tage, in der Früh, mit Streichen
Knirschender Äxte brachen Nachbarn ein
Und hörten Stille dort und sahen Leichen
(Und munkelten von einem grünen Schein

15
Der von Gesichtern ausgehn kann), auch roch noch
Verliebt das Bett, das Fenster borst vor Frost:
Ein Leichnam ist was Kaltes! Ach, es kroch noch
Ein schwarzer Faden Kälte aus der Brust.

LEGENDE VOM TOTEN SOLDATEN

1

Und als der Krieg im fünften Lenz
Keinen Ausblick auf Frieden bot
Da zog der Soldat seine Konsequenz
Und starb den Heldentod.

2

Der Krieg war aber noch nicht gar
Drum tat es dem Kaiser leid
Daß sein Soldat gestorben war:
Es schien ihm noch vor der Zeit.

3

Der Sommer zog über die Gräber her
Und der Soldat schlief schon
Da kam eines Nachts eine militär-
ische ärztliche Kommission.

4

Es zog die ärztliche Kommission
Zum Gottesacker hinaus
Und grub mit geweihtem Spaten den
Gefallnen Soldaten aus.

5

Und der Doktor besah den Soldaten genau
Oder was von ihm noch da war
Und der Doktor fand, der Soldat war k. v.
Und er drücke sich vor der Gefahr.

LEGEND OF THE DEAD SOLDIER*

1
The fifth spring came and still the war
No glimpse of peace supplied.
The soldier drew the consequence:
A hero's death he died.

2
But because the war was still going on
The Kaiser could only regret
That his soldier had gone and died on him:
He shouldn't have done that yet.

3
And summer swept over the many graves.
The soldier slept. And then
One night a deputation came
Of military medical men.

4
The medical deputation rode
Out to the soldier's grave
And dug God's little acre up
With a consecrated spade.

5
And the doctor examined the soldier
Or what of him was left.
And the doctor found him to be 1 A:
He must have been dodging the draft.

*Copyright © 1958 by Eric Bentley.

6

Und sie nahmen sogleich den Soldaten mit
Die Nacht war blau und schön.
Man konnte, wenn man keinen Helm aufhatte
Die Sterne der Heimat sehn.

7

Sie schütteten ihm einen feurigen Schnaps
In den verwesten Leib
Und hängten zwei Schwestern in seinen Arm
Und sein halb entblößtes Weib.

8

Und weil der Soldat nach Verwesung stinkt
Drum hinkt ein Pfaffe voran
Der über ihn ein Weihrauchfaß schwingt
Daß er nicht stinken kann.

9

Voran die Musik mit Tschindrara
Spielt einen flotten Marsch.
Und der Soldat, so wie er's gelernt
Schmeißt seine Beine vom Arsch.

10

Und brüderlich den Arm um ihn
Zwei Sanitäter gehn
Sonst flög er noch in den Dreck ihnen hin
Und das darf nicht geschehn.

6

And they took the soldier away with them.
A bright blue sky was on hand.
When you took your helmet off you could see
The stars of the Fatherland.

7

And into his decomposing corpse
They poured some alcohol
And hung two nurses on his arm
And his half-uncovered gal.

8

And because the soldier smells of rot
A priest with a limp does well
To wave some incense over him
So no one smells the smell.

9

The band goes BOOM-di-di-BOOM in front
As they play a snappy march
And the soldier, just as he has been taught,
Throws out his legs from his arse.

10

Their brotherly arms about his neck
Two first-aid men march on
Or he'd have fallen in the mud
And such things are not done.

11

Sie malten auf sein Leichenhemd
Die Farben schwarz-weiß-rot
Und trugen's vor ihm her; man sah
Vor Farben nicht mehr den Kot.

12

Ein Herr im Frack schritt auch voran
Mit einer gestärkten Brust
Der war sich als ein deutscher Mann
Seiner Pflicht genau bewußt.

13

So zogen sie mit Tschindrara
Hinab die dunkle Chaussee
Und der Soldat zog taumelnd mit
Wie im Sturm die Flocke Schnee.

14

Die Katzen und die Hunde schrein
Die Ratzen im Feld pfeifen wüst:
Sie wollen nicht französisch sein
Weil das eine Schande ist.

15

Und wenn sie durch die Dörfer ziehn
Waren alle Weiber da.
Die Bäume verneigten sich. Vollmond schien.
Und alles schrie hurra!

11

They painted on his winding sheet
The colors black-red-white.
This flag they raised, and because of the colors
The dirt was hid from sight.

12

A man in tails and a well-starched shirt
Was also out in front.
As a good German he knows exact-
ly what his countrymen want.

13

With BOOM-di-di-BOOM they strode along
Down the darkling lane
And the soldier reeled along with them
Like the snowflake in the gale.

14

The cats they squeal, the puppies too,
Field rats squeak lustily.
None of them want to be French, it's such
A shameful thing to be.

15

And when they marched through the villages
The womenfolk drew near
The trees bowed down and the full moon shone
And everyone joined in a cheer.

16

Mit Tschindrara und Wiedersehn!
Und Weib und Hund und Pfaff!
Und mitten drin der tote Soldat
Wie ein besoffner Aff.

17

Und wenn sie durch die Dörfer ziehn
Kommt's, daß ihn keiner sah
So viele waren herum um ihn
Mit Tschindra und Hurra.

18

So viele tanzten und johlten um ihn
Daß ihn keiner sah.
Man konnte ihn einzig von oben noch sehn
Und da sind nur Sterne da.

19

Die Sterne sind nicht immer da.
Es kommt ein Morgenrot.
Doch der Soldat, so wie er's gelernt
Zieht in den Heldentod.

16
With BOOM-di-di-BOOM and SEE YOU SOON!
Priest and gal and pups
And the dead soldier in the midst
Like a monkey in his cups.

17
No one could see the soldier now
There was so little room
So many marched and jostled him
With cheers and BOOM-di-di-BOOM.

18
So many danced and reveled there
The soldier could not be seen.
The stars could see him from the sky
Where no one's ever been.

19
And the stars aren't always in the sky
For lo! the dawn cometh!
But the soldier, just as he has been taught,
Marched to a hero's death.

SCHLUSSKAPITEL

CONCLUDING CHAPTER

GEGEN VERFÜHRUNG

1

Laßt euch nicht verführen!
Es gibt keine Wiederkehr.
Der Tag steht in den Türen;
Ihr könnt schon Nachtwind spüren:
Es kommt kein Morgen mehr.

2

Laßt euch nicht betrügen!
Das Leben wenig ist.
Schlürft es in vollen Zügen!
Es wird euch nicht genügen
Wenn ihr es lassen müßt!

3

Laßt euch nicht vertrösten!
Ihr habt nicht zu viel Zeit!
Laßt Moder den Erlösten!
Das Leben ist am größten:
Es steht nicht mehr bereit.

4

Laßt euch nicht verführen!
Zu Fron und Ausgezehr!
Was kann euch Angst noch rühren?
Ihr sterbt mit allen Tieren
Und es kommt nichts nachher.

DO NOT LET THEM FOOL YOU!

1

Do not let them fool you!
There is no way back home.
Day's on the point of going
Already the night wind's blowing.
No dawn will ever come.

2

Do not let them gyp you!
Life is not very big.
Drink it! And go on drinking
And when at last you're sinking
You'll want another swig.

3

Don't let them get your hopes up!
Today is all there is.
Let pious people suffer!
Life's all earth has to offer.
There's no life after this.

4

Don't let them lure you into
Exhaustion and duress!
Why all the trepidation?
You die like all creation.
And after: nothingness.

ANHANG

Vom armen B. B.

APPENDIX

On the Poor B. B.

VOM SCHLECHTEN GEBISS

1

Zahnlos von vielem Brombeernschlecken
Katzbalgerei und Zähneblecken
Unschuldig ein Kind, keusch wie ein Greis
Verfliegt mir mein Leben in solcher Weis':

2

Wohl zermalme ich Steine mit meinem Kiefer
Aber mein Zahnfleisch ist blau wie Schiefer!
Darum jeden Tag mit dem Gaumen gekaut
Daß mir das Pack in den Magen schaut?!

3

Viele Weiber trollten mit mir in Lumpen
Aber seit ich diese verfaulten Stumpen
Im Maul hab, bin für sie ich kein Mann
Der Fleisch einfach zerreißen kann.

4

Viele Jahre ging ich herum, einen Kiefer voll Zähne
Und es dankte mir niemals so eine Hyäne.
Jetzt seh ich, dessen Bild in ihren Hirnen schwankt
Daß ich alles nur meinen Zähnen verdankt.

5

Verachtet und boshaft, wurde ich mit den
                Jahren kälter
Und begab mich ganz auf die metaphysischen
                Felder.
Gemieden von mir, bin ich seit Tag und Jahr
Dem Schnaps verfallen mit Haut und Haar.

ON A BAD SET OF TEETH

1

Toothless am I from munching blackberries and
Showing my teeth and getting out of hand.
Naive as a child and as a dotard chaste
My life somewhat as follows runs to waste:

2

I crush stones with my jaws (first let me state)
But then my gums are blue as any slate
And if I do my chewing with my palate
Is it so the mob can stare right down my gullet?

3

The women ran around with me in rags
But with these rotten stumps in my mug the hags
Cannot see me as a man whose special art
Is to tear the women's meat apart.

4

For many years teeth filled up both these jaws
And those hyenas gave me no applause.
Now I, whose image wavers in their heads, confess
'Twas to my teeth I owed all my success.

5

Despised and spiteful, I cooled off later on.
My metaphysical exploits could then begin.
After long separation from myself
Hook line and sinker I succumbed to gin.

VON SEINER STERBLICHKEIT

1

Mir sagte der Arzt: Rauchen Sie ruhig ihre Virginien!
Um die Ecke muß schließlich mit oder ohne ein jeder.
In der Schleimhaut meiner Pupille z.B. sind krebsige
     Linien:
Daran sterbe ich früher oder später.

2

Natürlich braucht einer deswegen nicht zu verzagen
So einer kann noch lange leben.
Er kann sich den Leib voll mit Hühnern und Brombeeren schlagen
Einmal natürlich reißt es ihn eben.

3

Dagegen aber richtet keiner was aus, weder mit Schnaps noch mit
     Schlichen!
So ein Krebs wächst heimlich, ohne daß man ihn spürt.
Und womöglich bist du schon ausgestrichen
Und hast eben noch deine Braut zum Altare geführt.

4

Mein Onkel z.B. trug noch gebügelte Hosen
Als er schon lange gezeichnet war.
Er sah aus wie's Leben, aber es waren Kirchhofsrosen
Und an ihm war kein gesundes Haar.

5

Da gibt es Leute, die haben es in der Familie
Aber sie gestehen es sich nicht ein.

ON HIS MORTALITY

1

Smoke your cigars, go right ahead, the doctor told me,
With or without them everyone's gotta go—obviously.
In the mucous membrane of my eye there are, for example, traces of
        cancer:
Sooner or later they'll be the death of me.

2

A man need not, of course, despair on that account.
He may yet live long, he really may.
He can fill his stomach with chicken and with blackberries.
It's true he's going to have a bellyache one day.

3

Nothing can be done about it anyhow, either with drink or
        shenanigans.
Such a cancer grows imperceptibly inside.
It is possible you've already been crossed off the list
At the moment you approach the altar with your bride.

4

My uncle, for example, still wore well-pressed trousers
When he was marked for the kill.
He looked like life itself, but they were cemetery flowers:
Every hair on his body was ill.

5

There are people who have it in the family
Only they don't admit it, ever.

Sie verwechseln nicht Ananas mit Petersilie
Aber ihr Krebs kann ein Leistenbruch sein.

6

Mein Großvater wiederum wußte genau, was ihm blühte
Und lebte vorsichtig, peinlich nach dem Rezept.
Und brachte es so auf fünfzig Jahre; dann war er es müde
Aber so hätte freilich kein Hund einen Tag gelebt.

7

Unsereiner weiß: es ist keiner zu beneiden.
Jeder hat sein Kreuz, wie er immer war.
Ich selber habe ein Nierenleiden
Ich darf nichts trinken seit Tag und Jahr.

They know the difference between pineapple and parsley
But between cancer and a rupture? Never.

6

My grandfather, on the other hand, knew exactly what he was in for
And lived cautiously according to the doctor's fiat
And got to be fifty before he was sick of it.
It should happen to a dog, a life like that.

7

You and I know: no man is to be envied.
However he lives, each has his cross to bear.
I myself have kidney trouble and
Haven't been allowed to drink for many a year.

VON DEN SÜNDERN IN DER HÖLLE

1

Die Sünder in der Hölle
Haben's heißer, als man glaubt.
Doch fließt, wenn einer weint um sie
Die Trän' mild auf ihr Haupt.

2

Doch die am ärgsten brennen
Haben keinen, der drum weint
Die müssen an ihrem Feiertag
Drum betteln gehn, daß einer greint.

3

Doch keiner sieht sie stehen
Durch die die Winde wehn.
Durch die die Sonne scheint hindurch
Die kann man nicht mehr sehn.

4

Da kommt der Müllereisert
Der starb in Amerika
Das wußte seine Braut noch nicht
Drum war kein Wasser da.

5

Es kommt der Kaspar Neher
Sobald die Sonne scheint
Dem hatten sie, Gott weiß warum
Keine Träne nachgeweint.

ON THE SINNERS IN HELL

1

The sinners down in hell have
It hotter than you'd suppose
But if someone sheds a tear for them
Upon their heads it flows.

2

But they who burn most fiercely
Have none for them to cry
So on holidays they go begging
For some lymphatic eye.

3

But no one sees them begging
Through whom the cold winds blow.
One cannot see a man through whom
The hot sun's rays do go.

4

Along comes Muellereisert
In America he died.
His girl friend, who hasn't heard the news,
No water did provide.

5

Along comes Caspar Neher
As soon as night has fled.
Over him, God only can say why,
Not a single tear was shed.

6

Dann kommt George Pfanzelt
Ein unglückseliger Mann
Der hatte die Idee gehabt
Es käm nicht auf ihn an.

7

Und dort die liebe Marie
Verfaulet im Spital
Kriegt keine Träne nachgeweint:
Der war es zu egal.

8

Und dort im Lichte steht Bert Brecht
An einem Hundestein
Der kriegt kein Wasser, weil man glaubt
Der müßt im Himmel sein.

9

Jetzt brennt er in der Höllen
Oh, weint ihr Brüder mein!
Sonst steht er am Sonntagnachmittag
Immer wieder dort an seinem Hundestein.

6

And then comes Georgie Pfanzelt.
Unhappy are all such
Who like George Pfanzelt think that
They do not count for much.

7

After rotting in the hospital
Our little friend Marie
Is not bewept by anyone
And never a damn gives she.

8

And there in the light stands Bertolt Brecht
By a stone on which dogs piss.
He gets no water, because they think
He is in Heaven ere this.

9

He burns now in hell's fires.
O brothers mine, make moan!
Or he will stand on Sunday afternoons
Forever and aye by that dog-stone.

VOM ARMEN B.B.

1

Ich, Bertolt Brecht, bin aus den schwarzen Wäldern.
Meine Mutter trug mich in die Städte hinein
Als ich in ihrem Leibe lag. Und die Kälte der Wälder
Wird in mir bis zu meinem Absterben sein.

2

In der Asphaltstadt bin ich daheim. Von allem Anfang
Versehen mit jedem Sterbsakrament:
Mit Zeitungen. Und Tabak. Und Branntwein.
Mißtrauisch und faul und zufrieden am End.

3

Ich bin zu den Leuten freundlich. Ich setze
Einen steifen Hut auf nach ihrem Brauch.
Ich sage: es sind ganz besonders riechende Tiere
Und ich sage: es macht nichts, ich bin es auch.

4

In meine leeren Schaukelstühle vormittags
Setze ich mir mitunter ein paar Frauen
Und ich betrachte sie sorglos und sage ihnen:
In mir habt ihr einen, auf den könnt ihr nicht bauen.

5

Gegen abends versammle ich um mich Männer
Wir reden uns da mit „Gentleman" an
Sie haben ihre Füße auf meinen Tischen
Und sagen: es wird besser mit uns. Und ich frage nicht: wann.

ON THE POOR B.B.*

1

I, Bertolt Brecht, come from the black forests.
My mother took me to the cities while I lay
Inside her. And the coldness of the forests
Will be with me till my dying day.

2

The asphalt cities are my home. From the very first
They supplied me with every last sacrament:
Newspapers, tobacco, brandy. . . .
Suspicious, lazy, and, when all's said, content.

3

I am friendly with people. I stick
A bowler on my head as they do.
They are beasts, I say, with a particular odor.
So what? I also say, I am too.

4

In the morning, sometimes, I take some girls and sit them
In my empty rocking chairs. Whereupon I
Look them nonchalantly over and declare:
In me you have a man on whom you can't rely.

5

Toward evening I gather some fellows around me.
We address one another as: Gentlemen.
They put their feet up on my table and remark:
Things will improve. I don't ask when.

6

Gegen Morgen in der grauen Frühe pissen die Tannen
Und ihr Ungeziefer, die Vögel, fängt an zu schrein.
Um die Stunde trink ich mein Glas in der Stadt aus und schmeiße
Den Tabakstummel weg und schlafe beunruhigt ein.

7

Wir sind gesessen ein leichtes Geschlechte
In Häusern, die für unzerstörbare galten
(So haben wir gebaut die langen Gehäuse des Eilands Manhattan
Und die dünnen Antennen, die das Atlantische Meer unterhalten).

8

Von diesen Städten wird bleiben: der durch sie hindurchging,
        der Wind!
Fröhlich machet das Haus den Esser: er leert es.
Wir wissen, daß wir Vorläufige sind
Und nach uns wird kommen: nichts Nennenswertes.

9

Bei den Erdbeben, die kommen werden, werde ich hoffentlich
Meine Virginia nicht ausgehen lassen durch Bitterkeit
Ich, Bertolt Brecht, in die Asphaltstädte verschlagen
Aus den schwarzen Wäldern in meiner Mutter in früher Zeit.

6

Toward morning, in the gray dawn, the pines are pissing
And their bugs, the birds, begin to screech.
At that hour I am emptying my glass in the city:
I throw my cigar stub away and fall into troubled sleep.

7

We have been living, a light generation,
In houses that were thought beyond destruction.
(The lanky buildings of Manhattan Island and the fine antennae
That amuse the Atlantic Ocean are of our construction.)

8

Of these cities will remain that which blew through them,
        the wind.
The house makes the dinner guest merry. He cleans it out.
We know we're only temporary and after us will follow
Nothing worth talking about.

9

In the earthquakes that will come I hope I won't let my
Cigar go out in bitterness, though:
I, Bertolt Brecht, deflected from the black forests
Into the asphalt cities inside my mother long ago.

TUNES TO THE SONGS

Here are given all tunes printed in the 1927 edition of *Die Hauspostille,*
plus two others. The fourteen tunes printed in *Die Hauspostille* have
sometimes been attributed to Brecht.* However, one is assigned by
Brecht himself to an earlier source. This is the tune to the "Ballad of
the Pirates." Brecht calls the tune "L'étendard de la pitié." The present
translator has endeavored to trace it but without success. A distin-
guished French musician, Darius Milhaud, offered as his impression
that it is no folk song, as both Brecht and Paul Dessau have suggested,
but perhaps a show tune from the French theatre of the late nineteenth
century. One of the tunes printed in *Die Hauspostille* has obvious
components. This is the "Benares Song," which is made up of "There
is a Tavern in the Town" and "Un bel dí" from *Madama Butterfly.* The
two tunes added here to those previously printed with the poems are
the tune of the old German hymn "Lobe den Herren," of which Brecht's
"Grand Hymn of Thanksgiving" is a parody, and the tune of "Memory
of Marie A." As to the latter, the translator received an interesting letter
from a musician. It reads, in part: "This song was composed by a certain Umlauft about 1905. The title of the song is 'Verlorenes Glück.'
I found it in the catalogue No. 3245–46 (in an arrangement of L.
Mendelsohn for violin and piano) published by Adolf Kunz, Berlin.
The refrain goes like this:

> Verlorenes Glück, wie liebt' ich Dich mein Leben
> Ich hätt' geküsst die Spur von Deinem Tritt
> Hätt' gerne alles für Dich hingegeben
> Doch dennoch Du, Du hast mich nie geliebt."

—E. B.

---

*E.g., by Kurt Weill in his article "Gestus in Music" in *Tulane Drama Review,*
Autumn 1961.

Apfelboeck or The Lily of the Field

Apfelböck oder Die Lilie auf dem Felde

And   in   the   mild   light   Ja – cob   Ap – fel –
In   mil – dem   Lich –   te   Ja – kob   Ap – fel –

boeck   Struck both his   fa – ther and his   moth – er
böck   Er – schlug den   Va – ter und die   Mut – ter

down   And locked the   bod – ies   in   the   laun – dry
sein   Und schloss sie   bei – de   in   den   Wä – sche –

chest   And went on   liv – ing in   the house a – lone.
schrank Und blieb im   Hau – se üb – rig, er   al – lein.

Hymn of the Red Army Soldier

Gesang des Soldaten der roten Armee

Be-cause be - neath— a lead - en sun— This land of
Weil un - ser Land— zer-fress - sen ist— Mit ei - ner

ours— is gnawed a - way— It spat us out— on freez-ing
mat - ten Son - ne drin— Spie es uns aus— in dunk - le

high - ways It spat us out— on by - ways dark.
Stras - sen Und frie - ren - de — Chaus - se - en hin.

Hymn of Orge

Orges Gesang

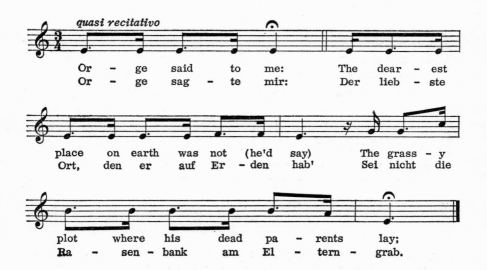

Or - ge said to me: The dear - est
Or - ge sag - te mir: Der lieb - ste

place on earth was not (he'd say) The grass - y
Ort, den er auf Er - den hab' Sei nicht die

plot where his dead pa - rents lay;
Ra - sen - bank am El - tern - grab.

Orge's Answer

Orges Antwort

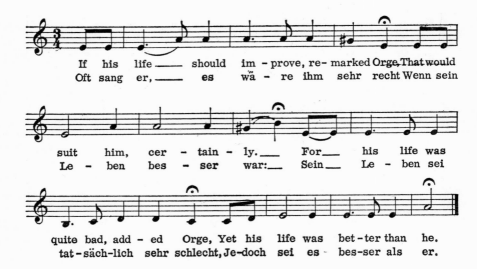

If his life——— should im - prove, re- marked Orge, That would
Oft sang er,——— es wä - re ihm sehr recht Wenn sein

suit him, cer - tain - ly.— For— his life was
Le - ben bes - ser war:— Sein— Le - ben sei

quite bad, add - ed Orge, Yet his life was bet -ter than he.
tat-säch-lich sehr schlecht, Je-doch sei es - bes-ser als er.

Grand Hymn of Thanksgiving

Großer Dankchoral

Praise ye the night and the   dark-ness of night all   a - round
Lo - bet die Nacht und die   Fin - ster - nis, die euch um - fang -

you!   All   ye, come nigh!   Look at   the   Heav - ens   on
en!   Kom - met   zu - hauf   Schaut in   den   Him - mel hin -

high!   Your day   is   al - read - y   o   -   ver.
auf: Schon ist   der   Tag euch ver - gang   -   en.

257

Ballad of the Adventurers

Ballade von den Abenteurern

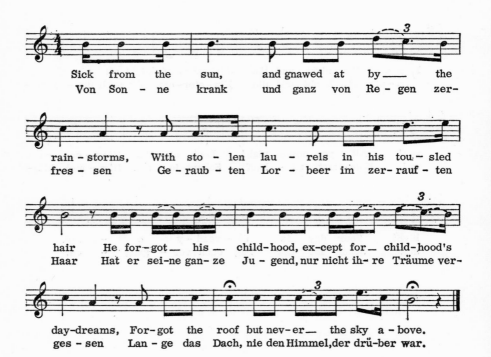

Sick from the sun, and gnawed at by ___ the
Von Son - ne krank und ganz von Re - gen zer-

rain - storms, With sto - len lau - rels in his tou - sled
fres - sen Ge - raub - ten Lor - beer im zer - rauf - ten

hair He for - got ___ his ___ child-hood, ex-cept for ___ child-hood's
Haar Hat er sei-ne gan- ze Ju - gend, nur nicht ih- re Träume ver-

day-dreams, For- got the roof but nev-er ___ the sky a - bove.
ges - sen Lan - ge das Dach, nie den Himmel,der drü-ber war.

Ballad of the Pirates

Ballade von den Seeräubern

De-ranged by drink and all the dark-ness Mangled by
Von Branntwein toll und Fin-ster-nis-sen! Von un-er-

frost in i-cy night Drenched by the rains, high in the
hör-ten Güs-sen nass! Vom Frost eis-wei-sser Nacht zer-

crow's nest They all saw vis-ions and turned white. Nak-ed and
ris-sen! Im Mast-korb, von Ge-sich-ten blass! Von Son-ne

sick, burnt by a sun which In win-ter they wished back a-
nackt ge-brannt und krank! (Die hat-ten sie im Win-ter

gain In scorch-ing fev-er, stench, and hunger Those who sur-
lieb) Aus Hun-ger, Fie-ber und Ge-stank Sang al-les,

vived sang this re-frain: Stare on, O sky of stream-ing
was noch üb-rig blieb: O Him-mel, strah-len-der A-

259

blue! Do, wind, the worst that you can do! To hell with
zur! E - nor - mer Wind, die Se - gel bläh! Lasst Wind, und

sky and wind if we ____ Com-mand the seas round Saint Ma- rie!
Him-mel fah-ren! Nur ____ Lasst uns um Sankt Ma-rie die See!

Memory of Marie A.

Erinnerung an die Marie A.

Up - on that day, a day of blue Sep -
An je - nem Tag im blau - en Mond Sep -

tem - ber, Si - lent and still be- neath a young plum
tem - ber Still un - ter ei - nem jung - en Pflau-men-

tree,___ I held my si - lent, still, and pale be -
baum___ Da hielt ich sie, die stil - le blei - che

lov - ed, And in my arms a gold - en dream was
Lie - be In mei - nem Arm wie ei - nen hol - den

she.___ And in the wide and love - ly sum - mer
Traum.___ Und üb - er uns im schö - nen Som - mer-

heav - ens There was a cloud, and long I saw it
him - mel War ei - ne Wol - ke, die ich lang - e

there.____ It was pure white and, oh, so high a -
sah ____ Sie war sehr weiss und un - ge - heu - er

bove us: When I looked up, it van-ished in the air.
ob - en Und als ich auf - sah, war sie nim-mer da.

Off to Mahagonny!

Auf nach Mahagonny!

Off to Ma - ha - gon - ny! The air is fresh and
Auf nach Ma - ha - gon - ny Die Luft ist kühl und

cool There's horse meat there and wom - an meat And
frisch Dort gibt es Pferd - und Wei -ber-fleisch Whis-

whis - ky, cards, and pool. Beau - ti - ful green
ky - und Po - ker - tisch. Schö - ner grü - ner

moon____ of Ma - ha - gon - ny, shine on us!
Mond____ von Ma - ha - gon - ny, leuch -te uns!

For be - neath our shirts to - day We have
Denn wir ha - ben heu - te hier Un - term

dough with which to pay For a great big laugh up -
Hem - de Geld - pa - pier Für ein gros - ses La - chen

on   your   great   big   stu –   pid   puss!
dei – nes   gros –   sen   dum –   men   Munds.

To Stay in Mahagonny, You

Wer in Mahagonny blieb

To stay in Ma-ha-gon-ny, you Need a-bout 5 bucks per
Wer in Ma-ha-gon-ny blieb Brauchte je-den Tag fünf

di-em. And if you work hard then you
Dol-lar Und wenn er's be-son-ders trieb

Need per-haps a wee bit ex-tra. They all were stay-ing
Brauch-te er viel-leicht noch ex-tra.— A-ber da-mals

at the time.— In Ma-ha-gon-ny's po-ker-drink-sa-loon.
blie-ben al-le In Ma-ha-gon-nys Po-ker-drink-sa-loon.

And they lost in an-y— case but They got something out of it.
Sie ver-lo-ren in je-dem Fal-le Doch sie hat-ten was da-von.

On the sea and on land ab-so-lute-ly ev-ery-bod-y's
Auf der See und am Land Wer-den al-len Leu-ten ih-re

quasi recitativo, parlando

skin is tak – en off him. Ev – ery – bod – y sits and
Häu – te ab – ge – zo – gen Dar – um sit – zen al – le

sells the skin off ev – ery oth – er bod – y. Skin's a
Leu – te Und ver – kau – fen al – le Häu – te Denn die

thing that at all times can be con – vert – ed in – to dol – lars.
Häu – te wer – den je – der – zeit mit Dol – lars auf – ge – wog – en.

266

God in Mahagonny

Gott in Mahagonny

On a gray morn-ing All a-mong the
An ei-nem grau-en Vor-mit-tag Mit-ten im

whis-ky God came to Ma-ha-gon-ny. God
Whis-ky Kam Gott nach Ma-ha-gon-ny Kam

came to Ma-ha-gon-ny. All a-mong the whis-ky We
Gott nach Ma-ha-gon-ny. Mit-ten im Whis-ky Be-

no-ticed God had come to Ma-ha-gon-ny. As
merk-ten wir Gott in Ma-ha-gon-ny.

spong-es suck up wa-ter Do you de-vour my grain from
Sauft ihr wie die Schwäm-me Mei-nen gu-ten Wei-zen

year to year? None of you be-lieved that I was
Jahr für Jahr? Kei-ner hat er-war-tet, dass ich

com - ing.   When I   do come, is the cup - board   bare?
kä - me;   Wenn ich kom- me jetzt, ist al - les   gar?

All the men of Ma - ha - gon - ny looked at one an - oth - er.
An - sa - hen___ sich die Män-ner   von Ma - ha - gon- ny.

parlando

Yes, ___ said the men ___ of Ma - ha - gon - ny.
Ja,   sag- ten die Män - ner von Ma - ha - gon - ny.

Alabama Song

Oh, show us the way to the next whis- ky - bar

Oh, don't ask why,___ oh, don't ask why,___. For we must find

the next whis - ky - bar For if we don't find

the next whis- ky - bar I tell you we must die! I

espressivo

tell you we must die! Oh! Moon___ of A - la - ba - ma We

now___ must say good - bye We've lost our good old

mam - ma And must have whis - ky Oh! You know why.

Benares Song

Chorale of the Man Baal

Choral vom Manne Baal

When in - side the white ma - ter - - nal womb grew
Als im wei - ssen Mut - ter - scho - sse auf - wuchs

Baal Large al - read - y .was the sky and still and
Baal War der Him - mel schon so gross und still und

pale Young and nak - ed and al - most mi - rac - u -
fahl Jung und nackt und un - ge - heu - er wun-der-

lous As Baal loved it when Baal came to us.
sam Wie ihn Baal dann lieb - te, als Baal kam.

On the Seduced Girls

Von den verführten Mädchen

When I'm old the Dev - il comes and takes me
Zu den seich - ten, braun - ver -sumpf - ten Tei - chen,

To the shal - low, marsh - y ponds and brown
Wenn ich alt bin, führt mich der Teu - fel hin - ab

Shows me the ___ re-mains ___ of drowned ca - dav - ers
Und er zeigt mir die Re - ste der Was - ser - lei - chen

parlando

Which up - on my guilt - y soul weigh down.
Die ich auf mei - nem Ge - wis - sen hab.

Legend of the Dead Soldier

Legende vom toten Soldaten

The fifth spring came__ and still the war No__
Und als der Krieg__ im fünf - ten Lenz Kei - nen

glimpse_ of peace sup - plied. The sold - ier__ drew_ the
Aus-blick auf Frie - den bot Da zog der Sol-dat sei- ne

con - se - quence: A he - ro's death he died.
Kon - se - quenz Und starb den Hel - den - tod.

273

NOTES

Hugo Schmidt

This is a copy, drawn by Ellie Schmidt, of the Caspar
Neher Fire and Water Man as shown in the 1927 edition of *Die Hauspostille*. Reproduced by permission
of Ellie Schmidt.

P. 1 *Hauspostille* (Manual of Piety).

A "Hauspostille" is a book of prayers, sermons, hymns, and other devotional literature intended for the use of laymen. The German word "Postille" was borrowed from the medieval Latin "postilla" during the sixteenth century. It is derived from the phrase "post illa verba sacrae scripturae" (after these words of the Holy Scripture), which introduced a sermon or a commentary following the reading of a Biblical text, usually a Sunday gospel or epistle. There were "Kirchenpostillen," used by the clergy, and "Hauspostillen," manuals of piety for use in the home. Use of these books was almost as widespread as of the Bible itself, and the expression "Bibel und Postille" was common in the centuries after Luther, whose *Kirchen- und Hauspostille,* a collection of sermons, appeared in 1527. The English title *Manual of Piety* is derived from New England tradition. Titles such as the following may be found in American library catalogues: Pious Devotions To Be Used On Several Occasions; The Family Sabbath Day Miscellany; Devotional Exercises, Chiefly Designed For The Use Of Families On The Sabbath.

On one of the last pages of the 1922 edition of Brecht's play *Baal* appeared a publisher's announcement: "By the same author: Die Hauspostille." The publisher was Gustav Kiepenheuer, Potsdam. Herbert Ihering asked Brecht in a letter of October, 1922, what the *Hauspostille* was and if he could have a copy. Brecht replied that it contained "ballads" and added that it had not yet appeared. Thus it is probable that most of the poems of the *Hauspostille* were written prior to 1922. It was not until 1926, however, that Kiepenheuer printed Brecht's manuscript, and even then—after many disagreements—only in a private edition of twenty-five copies with the title *Taschenpostille* (Pocket Manual of Piety). Almost identical with the *Hauspostille* that appeared the next year, it was intended for distribution among friends and was not for sale. In the *Taschenpostille,* the poems had the appearance of Bible verses: tightly arranged in two columns, with lines frequently split and continued flush with the left margin. Printed on thin paper with titles and numbers in red, gilded edge, and bound in soft black leather, it looked more like a miniature Bible than a lyric anthology. In 1958, the East German publisher Aufbau-Verlag brought out a facsimile edition of the *Taschenpostille*. A friend of Brecht's youth, Dr. Hans Otto Münsterer, who owns a copy of the original private edition of 1926, says in a letter that the facsimile edition really is identical with the original (of which we have never seen a copy) except for the omission of one poem, the "Hymn of the Red Army Soldier" (see note). It should be mentioned, however, that all future references to the *Taschenpostille* in the notes pertain to the facsimile edition, not to the original of 1926. Brecht's *Hauspostille*, published in Berlin by Propyläen-Verlag in 1927, was printed in a more conventional form. It also contained fourteen melodies perhaps written by Brecht, and a drawing by Caspar Neher, showing a gigantic monster with derby and rosary (see p. 276). An inscription in fractured Latin below the picture read: Iste erat Hydatopyranthropos / vivens Augustis vindelicorum / per unum saeculum / 1898–1998 / saeculum canticorum machinarumque / major nisi Hymmalaya [sic] / tamen certe monte blanco / caput benevolentiae integritatis / semper aequam servans mentem / pueris puellisque amicus / inimicis terror / A dextra orbis terrarum / a sinistra pauperum potaturumque [sic] refugium / in prospectu Himmalaya / luna ridens sub atlantico mare lucido / dedectus [sic] est iste a caspar neher a. d. 1925. (This was the Fire and Water Man, who lived at Augsburg for one century, 1898–1998, a century of songs and machines; [he was] greater than all but the Himalayas but certainly greater than Mont Blanc, the peak of benevolence and integrity, always of an equable mind, friend of both boys and girls, a terror to his enemies. To his right, the globe; to his left, a refuge for poor people and drinkers; in the background, the Himalayas; and the moon laughing above the bright Atlantic Ocean; dedicated by Caspar Neher, A.D. 1925.) Another Neher version appears here as the frontispiece. The Fire and Water Man, it seems, was a fanciful projection of Brecht himself. In a later group of poems dedicated to Neher, "An meinen Freund, den Maler" (To My Friend, the Painter, 1948), Brecht elucidated the name of Neher's creation: The Fire and Water Man was supposed to be resistant to fire and water. However, Brecht wrote, he did not prove himself. Even the wall on which Neher had painted him had vanished. (*Gedichte VII*, p. 28.)

Shortly before his death in 1956, Brecht revised the *Hauspostille* for inclusion in an edition of his collected poems. It appeared in the first volume, published by Suhrkamp in 1960. Brecht had dropped from the collection twelve poems: "Gesang des Soldaten der roten Armee"; "Prototyp eines Bösen"; "Vom François Villon"; "Orges Gesang"; "Über den Schnapsgenuß"; "Vom Tod im Wald"; "Das Lied von der Eisenbahntruppe von Fort Donald"; "Lied der drei Soldaten"; "Wer in Mahagonny blieb"; "Alabama Song"; "Vom schlechten Gebiß"; "Von den Sündern in der Hölle." He added eight others, all of them written during the twenties: "Der Herr der Fische"; "Von der Willfährigkeit der Natur"; "Lied der verderbten Unschuld beim Wäschefalten"; "Orges Wunschliste"; Über die Städte"; and three "Psalmen." Changes of interest in the remaining poems will be indicated in the notes. The edition of 1960 will be referred to as *Gedichte I*.

Brecht was fond of using religious terms as titles for his works. He called a group of prose-poems "Psalms" (among them are the three added to the 1960 *Hauspostille*) and referred to his poems "Vom Klettern in Bäumen" and "Vom Schwimmen in Seen und Flüssen" (both from *Hauspostille*) as "Evangelien" (gospels, evangels), according to Dr. Münsterer. (H. O. Münsterer, *Bert Brecht. Erinnerungen aus den Jahren 1917–1922*, Zürich, Arche, 1963, p. 63.) In the early twenties, at the time when most of the poems of the *Hauspostille* were written, Brecht also composed a cycle of straightforward, powerful Christmas poems (cf. *Gedichte II*, pp. 104 ff.). Brecht was an avid reader of the Bible. *The Threepenny Opera* (1928) teems with Biblical references. When in 1928 a Berlin magazine, *Die Dame*, asked him to name a literary work that had influenced him most, he replied: "You will laugh: the Bible." Despite the fact that Brecht consistently poked fun at people who interviewed him or asked him significant questions, the power and directness of his poetic language does indeed resemble that of Luther. (For an examination of the impact of the Bible on Brecht's work, see Thomas O. Brandt, "Brecht und die Bibel," *PMLA*, LXXIX, 1964, pp. 171–176 and Bernard F. Dukore, "The Averted Crucifixion of Macheath," *Drama Survey*, *IV*, No. 1, Spring, 1965, pp. 51–56.)

Throughout his career, Brecht was drawn to parody. His favorite targets were the Bible, the German classics, sentimental love songs, and folk poetry. Yet his attitude toward these models was not one of mocking buffoonery. Aside from a few exercises in sophomoric ribaldry, simple iconoclasm and blasphemy were sentiments too primitive to attract Brecht. It has been shown that his parodies reveal an ambivalent attitude toward the models. "Parody gave Brecht an opportunity of fulfilling an unconscious desire to emulate and follow these examples. Under the cover of ridicule he could indulge the 'high-minded,' even religious impulses, which his rational, cynical self would not allow him to acknowledge." (Martin Esslin, *Brecht. The Man and His Work*, New York, Anchor Books, 1961, p. 117.) Münsterer (p. 51) reports that Brecht and his circle were fond of using the forms of prayer and petition in their poems. They read the religious poems of the later Verlaine, and the pious verses of Francis Jammes (1868–1938), whose *Quatorze Prières* had been translated into German by the Expressionist poet Ernst Stadler. According to Münsterer, Brecht was especially fond of Jammes' "Prière pour aller au paradis avec les ânes" (Prayer to Enter Paradise With the Donkeys) from this group of poems. Münsterer himself reportedly had planned to write a "Christkatholisches Gebetterbuch für alle Anliegen und in noch so heiklen Lebenslagen" (Christian-Catholic prayer book for all petitions regardless of the delicacy of the situations). In his twenties, Münsterer states (p. 133), Brecht did not reject the Christian religion, but fought those who he felt corrupted it. Critics were aware of Brecht's complex attitude toward religion and took care not to dub his *Hauspostille* an exercise in blasphemy. Karl Thieme, for example, wrote an essay in the Catholic periodical *Hochland* (vol. 29, 1931/2) entitled "Des Teufels Gebetbuch?" (The Devil's Prayer Book?). He concluded that Brecht's work was not the devil's prayer book since it makes the reader ponder his own religious values. Though anti-Christian, he said, the book could not be called satanic. Thieme called Brecht an opponent from whom something could be learned, one who speaks the language of the Christian church, a man to be reckoned with.

In the following notes on individual poems, dates of origin or first publication will be given wherever possible. The best source of information on these is Walter Nubel's "Brecht Bibliography," part of which was printed in the second Bertolt Brecht issue of *Sinn und Form* (1957).

P. 8 *Anleitung* (Guide).

The "Guide" follows in tone, vocabulary, and arrangement the prefatory notes that usually preceded a true *Hauspostille*.

Bittgänge (Supplications). In Roman Catholic liturgy, "Bittgänge" also denotes more specifically the days of "Rogations," special supplication offered on the three days preceding Ascension Day (the Thursday which comes forty days after Easter).

Apfelböck, Farrar, Villon. Dr. Münsterer has kindly pointed out in a letter that Brecht's poem on Apfelböck deals with an actual person and event. Apfelböck was tried in Munich in 1919 at the age of thirteen for the murder of his parents. Details of the poem, such as the purchase of an azalea and the curiosity of the delivery man and the milk woman, were taken from the event. Dr. Münsterer recalls that Marie Farrar and her trial were also historical. Brecht's remarks on François Villon (1431– after 1463), the great French poet, are a playful attempt at mystification. Brecht pretends not to have been too familiar with any of Villon's poems. The opposite was true. He had come to know Villon's works in 1918 through the excellent translation of K. L. Ammer (pseudonym of Karl Klammer), first published in 1907. (Brecht did not know French well enough to read them in the original.) Some of the poems in the *Hauspostille* clearly show Villon's influence, and even more do five of the songs in *The Threepenny Opera* (1928): entire lines and more were lifted almost verbatim from Villon-Klammer. Because of this, Brecht was sued by Klammer's publisher, Zeitler (Leipzig), in 1929, and subsequently had to pay royalties to Klammer.

Exerzitien (Spiritual Exercises) is also the term used for a "retreat," meditations performed in seclusion by Catholic priests and laymen.

Gummimensch (India Rubber Man), a term sometimes used to describe a contortionist, here suggests a very tough, resilient type of person not unlike The Fire and Water Man. He is one who can resist severe punishment and will always snap back into shape.

Tagzeiten (Hours) are the canonical hours of the Catholic breviary (matins, lauds, prime, and so on). "Kleine Tagzeiten" (Little Hours) are prime, terce, sext, and none. They require shorter prayers than the other hours. It is perhaps impossible to convey in a translation the Scriptural character of a phrase such as "Es wird geben Tagzeiten des Andenkens" (There will be appointed hours of remembrance). Placing the infinitive "geben" next to the inflected verb "wird" (in English, the only proper place for it), instead of transposing it to the end of the clause, lends a Biblical cadence to the sentence.

Franz Diekmann, Frieda Lang. See note on "Die Ballade vom Liebestod" (The Ballad of the Love-Death), p. 308.

Christian Grumbeis. According to information kindly supplied by the mayor of Aichach, there is no record of a Christian Grumbeis in the city registry. Aichach is a town near Augsburg.

Taschenpostille (Pocket Manual of Piety). Since the same "Guide" preceded the private edition of the anthology in 1926, the term "Taschenpostille" was appropriate. Brecht obviously forgot to change this to "Hauspostille" for the 1927 edition. The slip is characteristic of Brecht's indifference in matters of typographical correctness, including spelling and punctuation.

Anhang. Vom armen B.B. (Appendix. On the Poor B.B.). In the *Taschenpostille,* the heading read "Vom armen Bidi" (On the Poor Bidi). "Bidi" was a nickname of Brecht's and occurs in several poems: "Bidi im Herbst" (Bidi in Autumn), "Anna redet schlecht von Bidi" (Anna Speaks Unkindly of Bidi), and "Bidis Ansicht über die großen Städte" (Bidi's Opinion on the Great Cities), all written in the twenties and earlier (cf. *Gedichte II,* pp. 27, 28, 111).

George Pfanzelt (the 1927 edition erroneously had "Pflanzelt"; he died in 1963), *Caspar Neher* (the painter and stage designer, 1897–1962), and *Otto Müllereisert* (who became a physician and whose signature appears on the medical bulletin of Brecht's death in 1956, died 1957) were Brecht's close friends. Münsterer's book contains a portrait of Brecht with Pfanzelt, Müllereisert, and another friend, Otto Bezold.

P. 14 *Vom Brot und den Kindlein* (On the Bread and the Little Children).

First printed in *Das Dreieck* under the title "Ballade vom Brod" in January, 1925. With its short lines reminiscent of German folk songs, the poem combines a number of stylistic elements. The diminutives "Kindlein, Stückelein, Gewürzlein" point to children's rhymes; certain abbreviations have a colloquial ring: "Stein" (instead of "Steine"), "gangen" (instead of "gegangen"); yet the verses are imbued with the serious fervor of a hymn. The custom of numbering each stanza was inspired by hymns in real "Postillen," but it was also observed by another of Brecht's models, François Villon.

In *Gedichte I,* the sixth stanza was omitted.

2. "Himmel" means "sky" as well as "heaven," a fact of some importance in a number of the poems. (The English has, of course, the same double possibility in its plural form: heavens.)

For a study of the motif of "Himmel" (and several others) in Brecht's early poetry see Bernhard Blume, "Motive der frühen Lyrik Bertolt Brechts." *Monatshefte* LVII (1965), pp. 97–112 (I: Der Tod im Wasser); pp. 273–281 (II: Der Himmel der Enttäuschten). The essay also contains a short bibliography of other critical studies in Brecht's poetry. One recent book-length effort should be added: Klaus Schuhmann, *Der Lyriker Bertolt Brecht 1913–1933.* Neue Beiträge zur Literaturwissenschaft, vol. 20. Rütten & Loening (East Berlin), 1964.

P. 18 *Apfelböck oder Die Lilie auf dem Felde* (Apfelboeck or The Lily of the Field).

This poem was first published as a song (music and lyrics) by Hardy in Worms in 1921, but the entire edition was confiscated and destroyed (cf. Münsterer, p. 174). The music is lost. Thematically, the poem is a "Moritat," a ballad-like narration of some crime. Crowds used to gather around street singers to hear the latest horrors. In Brecht's childhood, "Moritaten" could reportedly still be heard at the annual fair in his home town, Augsburg. Brecht revived the form successfully; the best-known example is the ballad of Mack the Knife in *The Threepenny Opera.* The tone of the Apfelböck poem, on the other hand, shows a tenderness that is foreign to the "Moritat." The Biblical subtitle, "The Lily of the Field," is justified by the poem's style and diction which conjure up an atmosphere of purity and innocence.

In *Gedichte I,* stanza 4 was omitted.

1. "Erschlug den Vater und die Mutter sein" (Struck both his father and his mother down): the uninflected possessive adjective "sein," and especially its position after the noun it modifies, is related to the realm of nursery rhymes and folk songs.

P. 24 *Von der Kindesmörderin Marie Farrar* (On the Infanticide Marie Farrar).

Ever since Goethe witnessed the trial of the infanticide Susanna Brandt in Frankfurt in 1771–72 and created the character of Margarete in *Faust I,* the tragedy of the unwed mother who turns against her child has held a spell over German writers. The theme often entails an accusation against social conditions that brought about the tragedy. The form of Brecht's poem may have been inspired by the *oraison* as used by Villon. The two-line refrain in each stanza is akin to the latter's *envoi.* In this poem, Brecht's dispassionate and factual language resembles that of a police report. In mentioning Farrar's guilelessness and insensibility in the "Guide," he was obviously referring to the apathy and indifference inherent in the girl's report. A number of Brecht's characters, at times even Mother Courage, exhibit the apathy of those whose senses have become dulled by excessive hardship. Brecht was fond of using the name Marie since it spans the distance between housemaids and Saint Mary: cf. Sankt Marie in "Ballade von den Seeräubern" (Ballad of the Pirates), and the poems "Prototyp eines Bösen" (Prototype of a Bad Man), "Erinnerung an die Marie A." (Memory of Marie A.), and "Von den Sündern in der Hölle" (On the Sinners in Hell).

P. 32 *Das Schiff* (The Ship).

Written probably in January, 1919 (Münsterer, p. 102), first printed in the *Berliner Börsen Courier,* January, 1924, in an earlier version. Next to François Villon, it was Arthur Rimbaud (1854–1891) whose literary tutelage young Brecht eagerly accepted. Rimbaud's poems had appeared in a German translation by Karl Klammer in 1907 (the same year in which Klammer brought out his Villon). "Das Schiff" may have been inspired, to some extent, by Kipling's "The Derelict" and "The Last Chantey," but it has a more direct model in Rimbaud's "Le bateau ivre" (The Drunken Boat). In Klammer's translation, the latter appeared as "Das trunkene Schiff." Two other poems in *Hauspostille* are reminiscent of "Le bateau ivre": "Ballade auf vielen Schiffen" (Ballad Aboard Many Ships) and "Vom ertrunkenen Mädchen" (On the Drowned Girl). Rimbaud's influence was equally significant in Brecht's play *Im Dickicht der Städte* (In the Swamp), written between 1921 and 1924. One character, Garga, quotes extensively from *Une saison en enfer* and *Illuminations*: see *Seven Plays by Bertolt Brecht,* Eric Bentley, ed., Grove Press, 1961, notes, pp. 11, 32, 63, 64.

In order to stay reasonably close to the German, rhyme and stanzaic form were dropped in the translation of this poem, as in "Die Ballade vom Liebestod" (The Ballad of the Love-Death).

P. 36 *Gesang des Soldaten der roten Armee* (Hymn of the Red Army Soldier).

Brecht sang this song as early as January, 1919 (Münsterer, p. 101). It was first printed in *Kunstblatt* (ed. P. Westheim) in 1925. Provided that any factual reference at all is intended in the poem, one may doubt that Brecht had in mind the Soviet Russian army. It is more likely that he was referring to the army of Kurt Eisner's socialist Bavarian Republic of 1918–19. This "Rote Armee," as it was called, was annihilated by the nationalist Free Corps and Reich Corps that recaptured Munich in May, 1919. Nevertheless, to the Stalinist Brecht of the later years, the Red Army Hymn became an embarrassment. According to Elisabeth Hauptmann, Brecht's longtime secretary and collaborator, and editor of *Gedichte,* Brecht "stamped out" the poem immediately after its appearance in the *Hauspostille*—if a poem that has been published can be "stamped out" (cf. *Gedichte I,* p. 207, notes). In August, 1951, Brecht wrote to the publisher Peter Suhr-kamp requesting him not to reprint the poem in a new edition of *Hauspostille* that was to appear that year. Suhrkamp complied. The poem was also omitted from the facsimile edition of the *Taschen-postille,* Aufbau-Verlag, 1958 (cf. introductory notes on *Hauspos-tille*), and from the *Hauspostille* edition in *Gedichte I,* where Miss Hauptmann did not even list it among the omitted poems. She says that eleven poems were omitted; the correct number is twelve.

Title. Dr. Münsterer writes that the original title was "Gesang der Soldaten der roten Armee" (Hymn of the Red Army Soldiers—plural instead of the singular) in the periodical *Kunstblatt* and also in the original *Taschenpostille* of 1926. In his book (p. 101), Münsterer gives an extra stanza which, he says in a letter, originally was the second:

> Und den Absinth und fauler Schlamm
> in dieser Straßen Kot ausspie,
> den fraß die Tabes in den breiten Schenkeln
> der Schwestern unsrer lieben Frau Marie.

which Eric Bentley translates:

> And those whom dope and rotting mud
> Spat out into these highways' filth
> Disease devoured between the thighs of
> Our Lady Mary's sisterhood.

In order to stay close to the German, here as throughout the poem, the translator has dropped the rhymes, but, to give the English a firm outline and make it fit the melody, he adheres strictly to the meter and does not add extra syllables *ad lib* as the German does. Hence the English is shorter than the German and occasionally a word or so is sacrificed, as the reader may note from a more literal translation of the above-quoted stanza: "Those who were spat out into the dirt of these roads by absinthe and rotten mud were consumed by tabes in the broad thighs of the sisters of our dear Lady Mary." Similarly in stanza 3 "from lips of ice" would literally be "from mouths in which ice cracked." And in the first line of stanza 4 "by night" is only implied in the English, whereas in the German it is stated.

P. 40 *Liturgie vom Hauch* (Liturgy of the Breath).

Brecht wrote this poem in reference to Goethe's famous "Wanderers Nachtlied," a lyrical masterpiece of eight lines conveying the sensation of peace in nature and man:

Über allen Gipfeln
Ist Ruh',
In allen Wipfeln
Spürest du
Kaum einen Hauch;
Die Vögelein schweigen im Walde.
Warte nur, balde
Ruhest du auch.

(On every hilltop is rest; in every treetop can be heard barely a breath; the birds are silent in the forest. Wait, soon you too will rest.)

Brecht's title derives from the fifth line. The form of Brecht's poem is that of antiphonal responses—devotional verse alternately recited or sung by the clergyman and his congregation. "Liturgie," used in the sense of such responsive readings, can also mean "litany." A section of four lines from Goethe's poem is used at regular intervals, with slight liberties toward the end of the poem. One may wonder whether Brecht interchanged Goethe's "Wipfel" and "Gipfel" intentionally or accidentally. Despite his notorious carelessness in such matters, Brecht would have caught the error, or would at least have quoted the line correctly by accident once or twice. Such an insistent error would be comparable to an English poet's misquoting, seven times in a row, "Forever wilt thou fair, and she be love." It is more likely that Brecht purposefully interchanged the words, and for a specific reason: the magic of Goethe's poem lies in its tranquil sound more than in the "meaning" the lines convey. Brecht never had much love for this type of poetry. By interchanging two like-sounding words, Brecht carried Goethe's intention to the absurd and thereby introduced a new level of parody: keeping the sounds of the poem unchanged, he wrote a line of nonsense ("In every hilltop / Barely a breath"). The poem was set to music by Hanns Eisler, *Lieder und Kantaten* (Leipzig, n.d. [*circa* 1960]),V, pp. 184–191). In its musical version, the confusion between "Gipfel" and "Wipfel" has been "set straight."

4. "die war kalte" (which was cold). The ungrammatical form "kalte" (instead of "kalt") rhymes with "Walde," reminiscent of Goethe's rhyme "Walde" with the archaic extended form "balde" (instead of "bald").

24. In *Gedichte I,* "So!" was replaced by "Und."

31. "rote" (red) was omitted in *Gedichte I.*

34. "die roten" (the red) was replaced by "alle die" (all the) in *Gedichte I.* The later Brecht had become sensitive to the use of the word "red" in his earlier verse.

37–38. These lines experienced an interesting evolution through different versions of the poem. The *Taschenpostille* had "Da kam einmal ein großer Lämmergeier einher" (One day along came a big lammergeier [a large, barbed vulture]). This version had the most plausible imagery: birds would be more likely the prey of a vulture than of a bear. In the 1927 *Hauspostille,* the line became "Da kam einmal ein großer roter Bär einher" (as in the present text). But it was a bear that came "from overseas"; its symbolical association with the Communist revolution could not have been strong in Brecht's mind. Münsterer (pp. 130 f.) reports that Brecht had no articulated political conviction at the time and on one occasion even referred to Communism as a disease that had to be eradicated. In *Gedichte I,* line 37 remained unchanged, but the second part of line 38 was changed from "denn er kam von überm Meer" (because he came from overseas) to "das brauchte er nicht als Bär" (being a bear, he didn't have to). Thus the bear, no longer of any embarrassing transoceanic origin, was cut down to a direct allegorical figure representing the communist revolution.

38–39. Between these lines the *Taschenpostille* had one additional line: "Doch der wußte Bescheid und ging nicht auf jeden Teer" (But *he* knew his way around and wasn't fooled by every cheap trick).

P. 50 *Prototyp eines Bösen* (Prototype of a Bad Man).

This poem may have been inspired in form and content by Villon's "L'epitaph en forme de ballade," a request to his fellow men

to be merciful and to pray for him. Villon wrote the poem while he
was in prison waiting to be hanged. Brecht followed the same Villon
poem more closely in Macheath's prayer for forgiveness in *The Threepenny Opera.*

4. "das veralgte Haar" (seaweed hair). Lit.: hair entangled with
seaweed and algae.

The last four lines follow both Villon's form of the *envoi* and
the request for prayer common in Catholic liturgy.

P. 54 *Morgendliche Rede an den Baum Green* (Early Morning Address to a Tree Called "Green").

First published in *Das Dreieck,* January, 1925.

Green. In the twenties Brecht frequently used English- and
American-sounding names. Some of his plays are set in America,
but, like Kafka's novel, *Amerika,* in an America of the poet's imagination. Later, Brecht was uneasy about his early fascination with the
adventurous New World. In *Gedichte I,* he changed "Green" to a
more German-looking spelling, "Griehn." Moreover, he rewrote the
poem completely, giving it a sociological undertone and making it an
allegory: the speaker praises the tree for having outlasted the dan-
gerous night through its "unrelenting flexibility" (a Marxist touch)
and for having grown so high amid run-down tenement houses
("Mietskasernen"—which in German literature regularly accompany
the cry for social reform). Trees are a recurring motif in Brecht's
work. Often they appear in cities, chopped down and dying (as in his
first play, *Baal*), or barely alive, as in the poem "Der Pflaumenbaum"
(The Plum Tree). The present poem has its close counterpart in
"Hypernaturalistisches Gespräch mit einem Baum im Winter" (Hyper-
naturalistic Conversation With a Tree in Winter), *Gedichte II,* p. 73.

Among the seven poems with English titles in the group *Aqua-
relles* by Paul Verlaine is one called "Green." (Others are "Spleen,"
"Streets," "Beams." The sound pattern seems to have been important
to Verlaine.) Brecht's "Green" may have been inspired by Verlaine's
poem. (On Verlaine's use of the word "green" see V. P. Underwood,
Verlaine et l'Angleterre, Paris, 1956, p. 108.)

P. 56 *Vom François Villon* (Friend Villon).

Written, according to Münsterer (p. 51), in the summer of 1918, soon after Brecht had come across Villon's poems. (For more details on Villon, see the note on the "Guide.") The tone of this poem closely resembles that of many of Villon's in Klammer's translations.

Title: "Vom." This form is a contraction of "von dem," implying that in the nominative case Brecht would have spoken of the poet as "der Villon," with the definite article preceding the name. In German this usage suggests a friendly, though unsentimental relationship with the person thus referred to, as well as a charming sense of informality. (Hence the English title, "Friend Villon.") In the *Hauspostille,* Brecht used this form frequently, as in "Ballade vom Mazeppa" and "Erinnerung an die Marie A." It is reported that Brecht spoke even of his wife, the actress Helene Weigel, as "die Weigel"—apparently to stay away from what would have appeared to him middle-class sentimentality.

2. "Er lernte früh den Stein auf andre schmeißen" (Early he learned to cast the stone at men). An allusion to an actual occurrence in Villon's life: in 1455, apparently in self-defense, he hurled a stone at a priest, Phelippes Chermoye, who was attacking him with a dagger. Chermoye died from his injuries a few days later.

3. Villon was involved in numerous knifings. At least twice he was sentenced to be hanged, the last time in November, 1462, for having participated in a minor street brawl. The sentence was commuted to banishment.

4. "der Seele Stolz" (his confidence). Lit.: the pride of his soul.

"Marterholz" (gallows). The verb "martern" (to torture) is etymologically as well as semantically related to "Märtyrer" (martyr). "Holz" is wood. In a religious context "Marterholz" is often used metaphorically for Christ's cross.

5. Nothing is actually known about the date or manner of Villon's death. Brecht has people die in the shrubbery also in "Vom Tod im Wald" (On the Death in the Forest) and in *Baal.*

P. 60 *Bericht vom Zeck* (Report on the Tick).

Münsterer (pp. 142 f.) reports that Brecht recited this poem on

December 2, 1919. The original title was supposedly "Ballade vom lieben Gott" (Ballad of the Dear Lord). Münsterer mentions a drawing he made in his diary of a tall man dressed in a long cassock, looking through a window into a room where a child, his hair on end, lies in a bed.

    1.   Violett. An allusion to the color of parts of the habits of priests.

    8.   In *Gedichte I,* "Haie" (sharks) was changed to "Säue" (pigs).

P. 66 *Vom Mitmensch* (On One's Fellow Man).

The ungrammatical title ("Mitmensch" instead of the correct dative "Mitmenschen") not only has a colloquial ring, but also conveys, with a curious impact, Brecht's irreverence even in the realm of language.

    5.   "netzen sie" (bless her). Lit.: sprinkle her.

Taschenpostille and *Gedichte I* have "Glied" (penis) instead of "Glück" (good fortune, here translated as "plaything"). "Glück," here, probably is a metaphor for "Glied."

    8.   The protagonist's "translating" his last words to his wife ties in with stanza 3 in which he had to learn to use the language of his fellow men.

P. 72 *Orges Gesang* (Hymn of Orge).

This song is part of Brecht's first play, *Baal,* in a slightly longer version and with one significant variant: in stanza 4, "wenn man erwachsen ist" (when you are old enough) appeared as "selbst in der Hochzeitsnacht" (even on your wedding night). *Baal* was to be published by Georg Müller in Munich in 1922. At the last minute, Müller decided otherwise and destroyed the plates. Münsterer (pp. 21 ff.) reports that Brecht had written the play within a short time in May, 1918, and revised it in 1919. On May 2 of that year (the day of the collapse of the short-lived socialist Bavarian Republic) Brecht read the new version to his friends. Only after further revisions, shortening and toning down the text, following the fiasco with Müller, was *Baal* finally published by Kiepenheuer, Potsdam, in 1922. An English translation by Eric Bentley and Martin Esslin was first published in Walter Sokel's *Anthology of German Expressionistic Drama* (Doubleday Anchor, 1963) and again in *Baal, A Man's A Man, & The Elephant Calf* (Evergreen Black Cat Book, 1964).

Orge is George Pfanzelt, mentioned in the "Guide," a friend of Brecht. Münsterer (p. 27) characterizes him as short, with a slight limp, and unpredictable: the "Mephistopheles of the circle." He was then a junior bank clerk, musically very gifted, and highly thought of by Brecht. An additional poem concerning George Pfanzelt appears among the pieces added to the *Hauspostille* in *Gedichte I*, pp. 69 f.: "Orges Wunschliste" (Orge's List of Wishes).

1. The first two lines paraphrase a sentimental nineteenth-century folk song: "Der liebste Ort, den ich auf Erden hab', / Das ist die Rasenbank am Elterngrab" (The dearest place I have on earth is the grassy plot of my parents' grave).

2. There is a play on words in German which the English does not carry over: Ort–Abort. The German for privy is "Abort" while "Ort," the mere stem of the word, means "place." In the Bentley-Esslin version of *Baal*, "Abort," in this poem, is translated "john." But the image which "john" conjures up is undoubtedly that of an up-to-date American bathroom, all tiles and porcelain and clean water, whereas the several "Aborte" in the *Manual of Piety* belong to the older world of wooden outhouses—the word "privy" is far likelier to suggest these.

8. Just as "verrecken" (see the notes on "Ballad of Mazeppa," p. 303) is a favorite Brechtian word for "to die," so a favorite Brechtian word for "to eat" is the brutal "fressen"—normally used only for animals. According to context it can be translated: feed, wolf down, bolt, devour.

P. 76 *Über den Schnapsgenuß* (About the Enjoyment of Gin).

Dr. Münsterer suggests that the poem, probably written in 1924, merely reflects an "alcoholic whim." Its factual impenetrability makes it reminiscent of the numerous experiments in abstract verse by some of the German Expressionist poets, except that in this poem Brecht seemed to convey a degree of intoxication through his use of the language.

1. "Aas" (carcass) is also a common term of abuse.

3. The sense of the original being far from apparent, the "sieben Sterne" have been taken as a brandy label like Five Star.

4. "wie'n Meier" (most sedately). Meier, the commonest of German names, suggests the ordinary, conforming citizen. The line "Ach du Schwan . . . , sei bedankt" (Thou swan . . . accept a cheer) was apparently inspired by Richard Wagner's line from *Lohengrin:* "Nun sei bedankt, mein lieber Schwan." The swan of Lohengrin was a favorite allusion of Brecht's. See also *Baal* and the notes to *The Three-penny Opera.*

P. 78 *Vorbildliche Bekehrung eines Branntweinhändlers* (Exemplary Conversion of a Brandy Peddler).

The poem follows in tone and even subject matter examples of the genre of "Erbauungsliteratur"—edifying, devotional literature with a strong moral message. It was set to music by Kurt Weill and became part of the musical play *Happy End* (1929) which Brecht wrote in collaboration with Elisabeth Hauptmann. Set in the Chicago gangster-land of pre-World War I, it deals with the efforts of a Salvation Army girl to mend the ways of a gang of criminals. They do, and finally join the Salvation Army. The play, performed in Berlin in the summer of 1929, turned out to be one of Brecht's most dismal failures. Eric Bentley's words were written for the Kurt Weill tune.

2. "wie Schleim" (like steam). Lit.: like slime.

4. "Algenlicht" (swamp-green light). Lit.: "algae-light." The image of algae is frequent in Brecht's early poems, as is the image of a swamp.

5. The last two lines read literally: He can see by (some) green spots that they are almost rotten.

P. 84 *Historie vom verliebten Schwein Malchus* (Malchus, The Pig That Fell in Love).

Dr. Münsterer suggests that the poem, probably written in

Berlin in 1924, was intended for recitation in a literary cabaret. No reason is known for Brecht's choice of the name "Malchus." There seems to be no allusion to the soldier Malchus in the Bible (the one whose ear was cut off by Peter) or to the Neoplatonist Porphyry (whose original name was Malchus) or to the Carthaginian senate leader of that name. It may well be a private allusion. On the other hand, the subject matter of the poem is reminiscent of the "Afrika-Politik" of Kaiser Wilhelm II, who claimed for Germany "a place in the sun," i.e., colonies in Africa. See Brecht's own comment on the poem in his "Guide."

P. 92 *Von der Freundlichkeit der Welt* (On the World's Kindness).

According to Münsterer (pp. 80 f.), written in 1917, or even earlier. Printed in *Uhu,* November, 1926. Hanns Eisler has set the poem to music. It is sung by Eric Bentley in the album "Songs of Hanns Eisler" (Folkways, FH 5433).

In *Gedichte I,* the third stanza was omitted, perhaps because of its comparative lack of quality (it contains the only two imperfect rhymes in the poem), perhaps because of the political dynamite in the sentence: "If you want to, you can go."

When Brecht, shortly before his death, reread the poems of the *Hauspostille* while preparing the *Gedichte* edition, he wrote a "Gegenlied zu 'Von der Freundlichkeit der Welt' " (Counter-Song to "On the World's Kindness"). In it, he questioned what he had said in the original poem and suggested that the world, at last, should be turned into a habitable place. (*Gedichte VII,* p. 122.)

P. 94 *Ballade von den Selbsthelfern* (On the Self-Reliant).

First printed in *Berliner Börsen Courier,* February, 1924, under the title "Ballade von den Männern im Holz" (Ballad of the Men in the Wood), with a few variants in the punctuation. The German term "Ballade" denotes both the French lyric form of the "ballade," practiced by Villon, for example (three stanzas of eight lines each in three rhymes, plus an "envoi" of four lines), and the "ballad," a simple story in verse, as in Percy's *Reliques of Ancient English Poetry.* This form of the ballad is also part of German literary tradition. Some of Brecht's ballad(e)s are inspired by Villon (although he never adhered to the strict form), others follow the ballad tradition, to which he gave an entirely new spirit and tone. But in many instances—as in the present poem—he used the term very freely, neither in the sense of a "ballade" nor in that of a "ballad."

2. "Herze" (courage): lit., heart. The poetically elevated form "Herze," instead of the more common "Herz," is within the tone of nineteenth-century heroic and patriotic literature. To the German reader, the form conjures up the atmosphere of false idealism familiar as the object of Nietzsche's attacks.

5. The term "self-help," connected with the German title "Selbsthelfer" (Self-Helpers), brings to mind Samuel Smiles's classic, *Self-Help.*

P. 98 *Über die Anstrengung* (On Exertion).

First printed in *Die Neue Rundschau,* December, 1923, in a somewhat different version, under the title "Ballade über die Anstrengung," and with a dedication, "für die Gerda Müller geschrieben" (written for Gerda Müller). In a letter, Dr. Münsterer writes that Gerda Müller was a friend of Brecht's. Concerning the diction of this poem, a statement by Brecht himself will be of interest. In a preface (written in 1954) to the first volume of his plays (Suhrkamp Verlag, 1957), Brecht explained his methods of composition in the early twenties: "I put together word mixtures like strong drinks, entire scenes in sensory terms depicting a certain consistency and color. Cherry pit, revolver, trouser pocket, paper god. Mixtures of that sort."

1. "befleckt" (defiles). Brecht punned with the idea of the immaculate conception, in German "unbefleckte Empfängnis." In stanza 9, he speaks of "befleckte Empfängnis" ("maculate" conception), tying it in with his use of "befleckt" in the first stanza.

3. "seit er die haarigen Hände entklaut" (into rude hairy fingers untwisting our claws). Lit.: "since it [brain, intellect] straightened out

('unclawed') our hairy hands." The image of straightening out claws suggests the incipient spiritualization of the human race.

P. 102 *Vom Klettern in Bäumen* (On Climbing in Trees).

Written in 1919 (cf. Klaus Schuhmann, *Der Lyriker Bertolt Brecht 1913–1933*, Berlin, 1964, p. 95), first published in *Das Tagebuch*, November, 1926. Münsterer (p. 63) reports that Brecht used to refer to this poem and the following one as "Evangelien" (see introductory note on *Hauspostille*) and that he had intended to add at least two more to the group.

2. The final statement, "Er wiegt ihn" (it has rocked it), bears more weight in German than can be rendered in English. Both "er" and "ihn" are accented, stressing the fact that it is the tree that rocks its top, and not vice versa. In English, both pronouns (for "tree" and "top") are "it."

P. 104 *Vom Schwimmen in Seen und Flüssen* (On Swimming in Lakes and Rivers).

See also the note on the preceding poem.

First published in *Der Neue Merkur*, November–December, 1921. The poem is somewhat related to Rimbaud's "Sensation" in diction and imagery.

P. 108 *Orges Antwort, als ihm ein geseifter Strick geschickt wurde* (Orge's Answer When a Soaped Rope Was Sent to Him).

See also the notes on "Orges Gesang."

According to Münsterer (p. 80), written in 1917, or even earlier.

1. The translation of the first line follows the German text given with the tune, and not as it appears in the poem ("Orge often sang").

3. To use the first half of a divided word in a rhyme (Täler, wähler-ischer) adds a witty nuance to the poem, especially if the word is divided incorrectly: the *r* should belong to the next line.

P. 112 *Ballade von den Geheimnissen jedweden Mannes* (Ballad of
the Secrets of Each and Every Man).

1 ff. "es ist nicht schad" (why not indeed). Lit.: It's no loss (to
kill him).

4. "vorm Haifischblicke dieser eigentümlichen Augapfelhaut"
(under the gaze of this extraordinary shark). Lit.: Under the shark-
gaze of this extraordinary cornea.

P. 116 *Lied am schwarzen Samstag in der elften Stunde der Nacht vor
Ostern* (Song on Black Saturday at the Eleventh Hour of the Night
Before Easter).

Black Saturday is the day between Good Friday and Easter
Sunday.

P. 120 *Großer Dankchoral* (Grand Hymn of Thanksgiving).

Printed in *Uhu,* November, 1926.

The hymn is patterned after the well-known church hymn "Lobe
den Herren" (Praise ye the Lord) by Joachim Neander (1650–
1680), schoolmaster and pastor in Düsseldorf and Bremen. (Like
Brecht's, it runs to five stanzas.) He was a Calvinist imitator of Luther-
an hymnody. The first two verses of Neander's hymn read:

> Lobe den Herren, den mächtigen König der Ehren,
> Meine geliebte Seele, das ist mein Begehren!
> Kommet zu Hauf!
> Psalter und Harfe, wacht auf,
> Lasset die Musicam hören!
>
> Lobe den Herren, der alles so herrlich regieret,
> Der dich auf Adelers Fittichen sicher geführet,
> Der dich erhält,
> Wie es dir selber gefällt!
> Hast du nicht dieses verspüret?
>
> (Praise ye the Lord, the Almighty, the King of creation!
> O my soul, praise Him, for He is thy health and salvation!

All ye who hear
Now to His temple draw near;
Join me in glad adoration!)

(Praise ye the Lord, who o'er all things so wondrously reigneth,
Shelters thee under His wings, yea, so gently sustaineth!
Hast thou not seen
How thy desires e'er have been
Granted in what He ordaineth?)

(English version from the Presbyterian Hymnal.)

Neander wrote his text, based on Psalm 103, to an existing melody which had appeared in the "Stralsunder Gesangbuch," 1665. Later, Bach incorporated the melody and Neander's text in his 137th cantata. Brecht wrote other hymns and chorales, the most notable being the six "Hitler-Choräle" of 1933 (see *Gedichte III,* pp. 37–49). They are patterned after well-known Protestant church hymns by Martin Rinkart, Paul Gerhardt, Martin Luther, et al. One of the six, "Bittet den Anstreicher, daß er den Zinsfuß uns senke" (Beseech the house painter [Hitler] to lower the interest rate), follows the same Neander hymn after which the present poem is patterned, and so does the "Iberin Choral" from *Roundheads and Peakheads,* "Bittet den Iberin, daß er die Mieten uns senke!" (Beseech Iberin to lower our rents). The hymn of the Salvation Army in *Saint Joan of the Stockyards,* "Sammelt mit Singen die Pfennige der Witwen und Waisen" (Gather the pennies of widows and orphans with song!) (cf. *Seven Plays by Bertolt Brecht,* p. 198), is Brecht's fourth, if somewhat freer, imitation of the Neander hymn. The original melody of the "Stralsunder Gesangbuch" is given among the tunes at the end of this edition.

"Großer Dankchoral" became part of Kurt Weill's cantata *Berliner Requiem.* A work for three male voices and wind orchestra, it was broadcast in the summer of 1929.

2. Lines 2 and 3 read literally: Behold, grass and beasts live like you.

5. "Schauet hinan" (Wake up and sing). Lit.: Look up (to heaven).

P. 126 *Ballade von den Abenteurern* (Ballad of the Adventurers).

Written, according to Münsterer (p. 19), in the summer or fall of 1917. First printed in *Baal,* 1922 (cf. the note on "Orges Gesang," p. 291).

1. "zerfressen" (gnawed at) implies "eaten away as if by a cancer."

2. "man war da" (one was). Lit.: one was there (in the sense of "existed").

P. 128 *Ballade auf vielen Schiffen* (Ballad Aboard Many Ships).

For Rimbaud's influence see the note on "The Ship" (p. 284).

1. "Laken" (sail). Brecht avoided the common word, "Segel," and chose "Laken," which means "sheet" and also "shroud."

2. "der nach nichts mehr fragt" (who'll . . . not ask why). Lit.: who doesn't expect much and will ask no questions.

5. "verfaulend ein Aal" (roasting and rotting). Lit.: like a rotting eel. The eel gains significance by virtue of a pun: "sich aalen" (lit.: "to eel oneself") is a colloquial idiom, meaning "to lie about lazily, roasting in the sun."

"Untergang" (sinking). Cf. note to stanza 8.

6. To the German reader, a "Marterpfahl" (stake) is inseparably associated with torture stakes in Indian tales and other exotic stories. On the further significance of "martern," see note on "Vom François Villon" (Friend Villon), stanza 4, p. 290.

8. The last two lines play on a paradox. "Versaufen" (more commonly "ersaufen") is slang for "to drown." "Untergehen," lit. "to go under," is a vague term connoting a number of ideas. It can mean "to sink," but also "to fall, decline, come to an end." On the literal level, "versaufen" and "untergehen" are almost synonymous. By contrasting the two terms, Brecht achieved a special effect: "versaufen" is a realistic, one-dimensional expression; "untergehen" has many overtones that point beyond the concept of sinking. The protagonist of the poem hopes for physical destruction, but he wishes to survive in a higher sense. In stanza 5, the term "Untergang" (the noun derived from "untergehen") refers to the ship: it faces its disaster, but the sailor moves on to a new ship.

P. 134 *Vom Tod im Wald* (On the Death in the Forest).

Written in the spring of 1918, according to Münsterer (p. 81). First published in *Der Erzähler,* a literary supplement to an Augsburg newspaper, *Die Augsburger Neuesten Nachrichten,* in March, 1918. It was also included in *Baal* (1922) and in the radio cantata *Berliner Requiem* (1929) with music by Kurt Weill. The American locale was introduced in the 1927 *Hauspostille* version. In the earlier version, in *Baal,* the first lines read: "Und ein Mann starb im ewigen Wald / Wo ihn Sturm und Strom umbrauste" (In the forest eternal a man lies dead, / Streams in flood below, winds screaming overhead) (Tr. from the Bentley-Esslin version of *Baal*). Originally, the poem did not contain any of the English terms (Gentleman, Prärien). Especially the fifth, sixth, and seventh stanzas were rewritten extensively for *Hauspostille.* According to information kindly furnished by the *Mississippi Valley Historical Review,* Indiana University, there is no Hathoury Forest in the Mississippi Valley. Brecht either invented the name or took it from some juvenile adventure story, perhaps a novel by the German author Karl May.

5, 6. Gentleman. Young Brecht used the English term frequently. (Cf. also "The Ballad of Hannah Cash" and "On the Poor B.B.") It adds a foreign, exotic flavor to his verse, but also conveys an ironic impact: belonging to the realm of the bourgeois, it clashes with that of the early Brechtian hero. Caspar Neher's representation of the "Fire and Water Man" captured this dichotomy by having his Mongoloid monster wear a bowler, cuff links, creased pants, and striped socks. Mack the Knife (*The Threepenny Opera*) is another of Brecht's "gentlemen."

P. 138 *Das Lied von der Eisenbahntruppe von Fort Donald* (The Song of the Fort Donald Railroad Gang).

This was the first poem of the *Hauspostille* to be published. It appeared in a somewhat different version in *Der Erzähler* in July, 1916, and again in the *Berliner Börsen Courier* in January, 1924. There never was a Fort Donald in Ohio.

Dr. Münsterer suggests that Brecht may have had sources for this poem and the next. Toward the end of the nineteenth century many news reports about events in the New World appeared in German papers. Often they turned out to be untrue or grossly exaggerated, but they nevertheless inspired literary creations at times. Dr. Münsterer mentions as the most outstanding example Theodor Fontane's famous poem "John Maynard," about the heroic helmsman who steered a burning boat across Lake Erie and died, the only victim, at the end of the voyage. In reality, Maynard's name was Fuller and he was among the survivors.

4. "das nasse Ohio wuchs unten" (below them rose this wet Ohio). The neuter "Ohio" refers to the state, not to the river (also in stanza 5).

In the version of 1916, the song sung by the men was not "Oh, wo ist mein Johnny zur Nacht," but "Näher, mein Gott, zu dir" (Nearer, my God, to Thee), the hymn sung by the passengers of the sinking "Titanic" in 1912.

P. 142 *Ballade von des Cortez Leuten* (Ballad of Cortez' Men).

Written probably in 1919, possibly earlier, according to Münsterer (p. 81). First printed in *Feuerreiter* in December, 1922. In *Gedichte I,* Brecht regularized the verb forms very effectively: in lines 1–15, all verbs in the past tense; 16–34, present tense; 35–51, past tense. Thus the section describing the men's frantic efforts to free themselves was put in the present tense, the rest of the poem in the past. In the present version, tenses are mixed indiscriminately. No historical event is known that could have inspired the theme of this poem. But cf. the notes on the preceding poem.

Seven lines from the end: "sie sangen sich wohl zu" (they were singing for one another). The line implies that the men sang in order to signal to one another for contact and encouragement.

P. 146 *Ballade von den Seeräubern* (Ballad of the Pirates).

Written in the summer of 1918 (Münsterer, p. 81), first published in the *Berliner Börsen Courier,* April, 1923. Possibly Kipling's "In the Matter of One Compass" inspired this poem, particularly in its rhythm. Kipling's refrain to the first stanza reads: "Oh, drunken

Wave! Oh, driving Cloud! / Rage of the Deep and sterile Rain, / By Love upheld, by God allowed, / We go, but we return again!"

"Sankt Marie" could point to a number of places, but it probably originated in Brecht's imagination. See also the note for "On the Infanticide Marie Farrar" (p. 284).

1. "Enormer Wind, die Segel bläh!" (Do, wind, the worst that you can do). Lit.: Enormous wind, swell the sails!

2. "vor dem Knall" (before the morning). Lit.: before the shot —most likely the shot fired from a ship as a signal for the sailors to re-embark.

Possibly the poem is a Brechtian retort to certain revolutionary songs, and specifically the "Marseillaise" and the "Internationale." Brecht calls the tune "L'étandard de la pitié," a phrase that may have a parodistic relation to "L'étendard sanglant est levé." The opening lines of the "Internationale" are: "Debout les damnés de la terre / Debout les forçats de la faim." Brecht's ballad could embody the same attitude to revolution as the "Hymn of the Red Army Soldier." (This interpretation is in part suggested by a letter from Dr. Münsterer, though it is not necessarily endorsed by him.)

P. 156 *Lied der drei Soldaten* (Song of the Three Soldiers).

This poem became the "Kanonensong" in *The Threepenny Opera* (1928) with music by Kurt Weill. To each stanza was added an eight-line refrain, the names were switched, and the wording of several lines was changed. The poem was also used in Eric Bentley's version of *A Man's A Man*, under the title "Song of the Scum," with music by Joseph Raposo. The title was perhaps suggested by Kipling's "Soldiers Three."

P. 158 *Ballade von der Hanna Cash* (Ballad of Hannah Cash).

Printed in *Die Neue Zeit,* April, 1927.

4. "kamen sich näher" (closer came) and "gingen vereint durchs Leben" (one life the other joins). Here the German suggests the language of the Spießbürger (petit bourgeois) or of the literature be-

loved by him. There being no exact equivalent of the cultural complex, the English here attempts only to convey a sense of literary language, "poetic diction."

6. "Savann." To the German reader, a savanna is a hopelessly remote, exotic place.

P. 164 *Erinnerung an die Marie A.* (Memory of Marie A.).

Written probably in 1919 (Münsterer, p. 102). First printed in *Junge Dichter vor die Front,* December, 1924.

Marie A.: When this name is pronounced, it comes to sound like "Maria," that form of the name which is always used in connection with the Virgin Mary in German. It is possible that Brecht consciously played with this effect. Cf. the note on "On the Infanticide Marie Farrar" (p. 284).

Concerning the tune of this poem, see the prefatory notes to *Tunes to the Songs.* Dr. Münsterer recalls that Marie A. was an actual person, either the daughter of a hairdresser or a girl working in a beauty parlor.

1. "die ich lange sah" (and long I saw it there). Eric Bentley states that he has sometimes heard another version of this phrase sung, thus: "die ich nicht lang sah" (I did not see it for long). The exact origin of this variant reading is not known. On his record, *Bentley on Brecht* (Folkways, FH 5434), Eric Bentley sings a translation of this apocryphal version: "I saw it fleetingly."

"war sie nimmer da" (it vanished in the air). Lit.: it was no longer there.

P. 166 *Ballade vom Mazeppa* (Ballad of Mazeppa).

Written probably in 1916 (Münsterer, p. 80), first published in the *Berliner Börsen Courier,* July, 1923. Ever since Voltaire's discussion of the Cossack leader's career in his *Histoire de Charles XII* (1731), Mazeppa (1644?–1709) and his famous ride have been a frequent subject in literature. There are Mazeppa poems by Byron, Victor Hugo, and, more recently, by Roy Campbell. Several minor German writers of the nineteenth century wrote novels and plays about him. Brecht's poem is the only version in which, contrary to historical fact, Mazeppa dies during his ride. Factually, he became a "hetman" of the Ukrainians and later allied himself to Charles XII of Sweden against the Russian czar, Peter the Great.

1. "verstrickt" (bound). The stem of the word, "Strick," means "rope," but normally "verstrickt" is used only figuratively, in the sense of "inseparably and fatefully tied to." Brecht's use of the term plays on the physical as well as on the figurative meaning.

7. "verrecken" (finish). Ordinarily, this term—very common in Brecht—would be used when referring to animals only. Applied to people, it has an extremely coarse ring. The English "croak" would be right in some contexts but not here.

"das lebende Aas" (living meat). Lit.: living carcass. Brecht sustained the animal image which he initiated with his use of "verrecken" in the preceding line.

8. The verb "sich sträuben" (stiffened and bristled) has a second, figurative meaning: to refuse to go along, to offer resistance. Again, Brecht used the term with poetic ambiguity.

P. 172 *Ballade von der Freundschaft* (Ballad of Friendship).

First printed in *Europa Almanach,* ed. by Carl Einstein and Paul Westheim, Potsdam, Kiepenheuer, 1925.

The poem may reflect the relationship between Rimbaud and Verlaine. In Brecht's own works, analogues are to be found in *Baal, In the Swamp,* and the story "Bargan läßt es sein."

P. 180 *Die Ballade von dem Soldaten* (The Ballad of the Soldier).

The same later version of this poem was used in *Mother Courage and Her Children* as in *Gedichte I.* In the table of contents of the *Taschenpostille,* there is a parenthetical note next to the title of the poem: "After an English soldier's ballad." No direct model could be found, but Kipling's "Ford O'Kabul River" and "The Widow's Party" may have inspired Brecht in terms of motifs and rhythmic patterns. The poem was set to music by Paul Dessau (as part of *Mother Cour-*

age) and by Hanns Eisler. The latter version is heard on *Bentley on Brecht*.

3. "es geht übel aus" (you'll end in the sky). Lit.: you'll end badly.

4. "mit dem Messer im Gurt" (he took up his sword). Lit.: with the knife in his belt.

"Mongefluß (Monge River) became "Schindeldach" (shingle roof) in *Gedichte I* and in *Mother Courage*. This change is part of Brecht's later tendency to strip his poems of their unreal, exotic setting. Attempts to locate a Monge River have been unsuccessful. In the musical setting of this poem by Hanns Eisler, "Mongefluß" was replaced by "Wolgafluß" (Volga River). Cf. Hanns Eisler, *Lieder und Kantaten*, I, p. 88.

5. "Wärme" (Warm air). Lit.: warmth.

7. "des Weibes Rat" (the woman's advice) became "des Weisen Rat" (advice of the wise) in *Gedichte I* and *Mother Courage*.

P. 186 *Mahagonnygesänge* (Mahagonny Songs).

This group of poems, originally published in the *Taschenpostille* and the *Hauspostille*, was set to music by Kurt Weill. He made up his own tunes, disregarding Brecht's (see Appendix, *Tunes to the Songs*). Weill's "Songspiel" *Mahagonny*, a kind of operatic cantata consisting of the five songs and an additional finale, was first performed at the Baden-Baden festival of modern music in the summer of 1927. This cantata, often referred to as the "Kleine Mahagonny" (Small Mahagonny), became the germ of the full-length opera, *Rise and Fall of the City of Mahagonny*, published in 1929 and first performed in 1930. The playwright Arnolt Bronnen, a friend of Brecht's in the twenties, reports that Brecht coined the term "Mahagonny" in 1923 having in mind the uniforms of Hitler's Storm Troopers who could be seen in the streets of Munich; "masses of petit-bourgeois, wooden figures in brown shirts . . ." (Arnolt Bronnen, *Tage mit Bertolt Brecht*, Vienna, 1960, p. 143). Later on, Bronnen states, the term received a different emphasis; but originally it bespoke for Brecht a "utopia of the philistine," a "cynical, stupid beerhall state." Dr. Münsterer questions Bronnen's explanation and avers that the word was used prior to the existence of the Storm Troopers. He suggests that Brecht liked the word simply for its rich sound. The word has to be pronounced with the accent on the short, open *o*. It is similar to, but not identical with, the term for mahogany wood: in German "Mahagoni," with a long, closed *o*-sound.

Mahagonny existed in Brecht's fantasy only. It is part of the mythical America that had an important place in the imagination of the young poet. Brecht's English lyrics are in the idiom of one who has listened to American jazz singers without really knowing English. In the *Taschenpostille*, the two English poems were even farther removed from our normal idiom than in the *Hauspostille*. The original "Benares Song," for example, had: "There is no girl to shake with hands" and "There is no great fun on this star." The rhyme Alabama / mamma is highly un-American. In the Columbia recording of *Mahagonny*, the refrain of the "Benares Song" is corrupted to: "Worst of all, Benares / Is said to have been perished in an earthquake!" Brecht's English is a language of its own; yet his German is at times just as uncommon.

In *Gedichte I,* Brecht omitted the second Mahagonny Song and the Alabama Song, but added to the group three "Psalms," composed in Biblical prose. He made several changes in the Benares Song, some of which are obviously meant to improve the English. ("Is here no telephone?" became "Is there no telephone?"). Others concerned content: "Johnny" became "Jenny," and the first line of the second stanza now reads: "There is no money in this town / The whole economy has broken down."

The Benares and Alabama songs were written in 1925, according to Elisabeth Hauptmann (cf. *Gedichte II,* pp. 256 f.).

P. 208 *Choral vom Manne Baal* (Chorale of the Man Baal).

This poem exists in a number of versions. Originally it appeared in Brecht's first play, *Baal* (1922), in a version of fourteen stanzas as opposed to the nine in *Hauspostille*. For a translation see Eric Bentley's

Baal, Evergreen Black Cat Books, 1964, pp. 20 f. In Brecht's 1957 edition of *Baal* in the first volume of his *Stücke* (Plays), the poem runs to eighteen stanzas. The author asserts in a preface that the "Choral" appears as it did in the "very first version" of the play; this seems to refer to the manuscript version of the play of 1918 (cf. the note on "Orges Gesang"). The same longer version of eighteen stanzas is in *Gedichte I.* Brecht made no changes in the remaining nine stanzas which he used in the *Hauspostille* of 1927 (and which appear in this edition). Münsterer (p. 84) reports that this song was Brecht's own favorite in his Augsburg days and that he recited it more often than any of the others. There has been much speculation concerning the name "Baal." Max Högel (*Bertolt Brecht, ein Porträt,* Augsburg, 1962, p. 19) remembers what he calls a life-size picture of Baal, the Semitic Phoenician deity of insatiability, in Brecht's room in Augsburg; others refer to the same picture as a "Syrian Earthgod." Münsterer (p. 24) expressly states that he remembers no such drawing and suspects that others may have mistaken Caspar Neher's cartoons of bigheaded Mongoloid "Verlaine-types" for representations of the god Baal. The 1922 edition of *Baal* has one such cartoon on the cover: this one, carrying a guitar, is obviously Brecht's Baal and not the Phoenician deity. A possible source for the name may be the Baal in Georg Heym's poem "God of Cities," or even Kipling's poem "O Baal, Hear Us." In 1926, Brecht asserted that his Baal was patterned after an actual character, a mechanic named "Josef K." (Kafka's *Trial* had appeared the year before; a facetious allusion on Brecht's part is not out of the question.) In the revised "Guide" to the *Hauspostille* in *Gedichte I,* Brecht wrote: "The first chapter [of the fifth lesson] is dedicated to the memory of the lyric poet Joseph Baal from Pfersee, a thoroughly asocial character." These may well be attempts at mystification. It is a fact that Brecht wrote *Baal* as a reply of sorts to a drama, *Der Einsame* (The Lonely One, 1917), by Hanns Johst, later a Nazi poet. It concerned the life of the nineteenth-century dramatist Christian Dietrich Grabbe. Also see the introduction to *Baal,* "Bertolt Brecht's First Play," by Eric Bentley.

P. 212 *Von den verführten Mädchen* (On the Seduced Girls).

3. The adjective "faul" has two meanings: "rotting" as well as "lazy." Brecht played on both connotations. Cf. "lässig und müde" (tired and lazy) in stanza 2.

4. The suffixed noun "Faulheit" would normally mean "laziness," but in this instance Brecht used it ambiguously to contain also the sense of "rottenness."

P. 214 *Vom ertrunkenen Mädchen* (On the Drowned Girl).

This poem appeared in *Baal* (1922) and was also printed in *Die Weltbühne* in November, 1922. Later, it was set to music by Kurt Weill and became part of the radio cantata *Berliner Requiem* (1929). Lotte Lenya sings the song on her "Berlin Theatre Songs" album (Columbia, ML 5056). The poem was no doubt inspired by Rimbaud's "Ophélie." On the influence of this poem on German literature, see Bernhard Blume, "Das ertrunkene Mädchen: Rimbaud's 'Ophélie' und die deutsche Literatur," *Germanisch-romanische Monatsschrift* XXXV (1954), 108–119. A number of poems in the *Hauspostille* contain the motif of decaying bodies or ships floating down a river.

4. "verfault war" (rotted). Lit.: had rotted.

P. 216 *Die Ballade vom Liebestod* (The Ballad of the Love-Death).

Dr. Münsterer recalls that the subject matter of this poem portrays an actual occurrence in Augsburg in 1918 or 1919. The names may or may not be historical.

The expression "Liebestod" (love-death) is closely associated with heroic-romantic literature, especially with Richard Wagner's *Tristan und Isolde*.

2. "in Hölzer sie gepfercht" (they are . . . hemmed in). Lit.: "they are crammed into wood"—perhaps the "closet" of stanza 11.

4. "verschwemmt" (moist and bloated), a neologism of Brecht's, conveys at once the two dominant metaphors of the poem: moisture and disease. There is a word "aufgeschwemmt" (swollen, bloated), and there is a "verschwimmen" (to blur, dissolve). Brecht combined

these two words, creating a new one. The stem "schwim-" or "schwem-" associates both expressions with the images of moisture and water.

6. "halbersoffne" (half-submerged in water). Lit.: half-drowned.

7. "hüllen" (hide) also means "to wrap."

9. "Tapetengruft" (wallpaper grave). Perhaps an allusion to Heinrich Heine's "Matratzengruft," (mattress grave) as he called the room to which he was confined during the last ten years of his life, suffering from paralysis.

11. "im verfaulten Schrank" (in the decaying closet). It is possible that Brecht imagined the couple in a tall wooden chest or wardrobe turned over on its back to serve as a bedstead.

P. 222 *Legende vom toten Soldaten* (Legend of the Dead Soldier).

Münsterer (p. 101) reports that Brecht sang this song early in 1919. He quotes a final verse not included in the published version:

> Es hat ein jeder Stand seine Pflicht.
> Die Musiker machen Radau.
> Der Pfarrer macht ein frommes Gesicht
> und die Ärzte machen k.v.

Eric Bentley translates:

> Every profession must do its stuff.
> The musician booms and brays.
> The Parson contributes a pious face
> And the doctors contribute One-A's.

The poem was first printed as an epilogue to Brecht's second play, *Trommeln in der Nacht* (Drums in the Night), 1922. Apparently written toward the end of World War I, it is often considered a direct outgrowth of Brecht's experiences as a medic—the customary assignment of drafted medical students—in the Augsburg military hospital in 1918. In an interview with the Russian poet Sergei Tretyakov, published in *International Literature,* Moscow, May, 1937, Brecht had told hair-raising stories of his experiences in that hospital, claiming that he, the first-semester medical student, spent his days casually amputating limbs and performing delicate trepanations. Critics have echoed this story ever since. Now Münsterer (pp. 94 ff.), an eyewitness, has shown that during the interview Brecht had merely indulged in his favorite sport: leg-pulling. In the Augsburg "military hospital"— a few wooden barracks in the courtyard of a public school—nothing but venereal diseases were treated, and Brecht's duties were never clearly defined. His superior spent most of his time over a microscope, and Brecht passed his time entertaining the patients with songs and poems. He reportedly wrote special pieces for them, including a "Song About the Cavaliers in Station D." He even charmed his superior into letting him live at home. Once he was rebuked mildly: he had decided to take a day off and sent his parents' cook to report at the hospital in his place. With or without legends about its origin, the "Legend of the Dead Soldier" quickly became Brecht's most famous and, in the eyes of some, his most notorious poem. It gained him a place on the black list of the Nazi party as early as 1923. In June, 1935, as author of the "Legend," he was deprived of his German citizenship.

3.   A "militärische ärztliche Kommission" (deputation of military medical men) consists of the medical representatives of the draft board.

5.   "k.v." (1-A) is the abbreviation for "kriegsverwendungsfähig" (fit for active service).

11.   "Und trugen's vor ihm her" (This flag they raised). Lit.: And carried it before him.

12.   The third and fourth lines read literally: "As a good German, he knows what his duty is." The entire phrase reflects the idiom of nationalistic rhetoric. (The expression "ein deutscher Mann" could not be used in any other context.)

P. 232 *Gegen Verführung* (Do Not Let Them Fool You!).

This song, probably written in 1918, was, according to Münsterer (pp. 139 f.), originally part of a play, *Sommersinfonie* (Summer Symphony). Written in 1919, the play was never published by Brecht. Its theme was the story of the matron of Ephesus (first presented in Petronius' satires and used as late as 1946 by Christopher Fry in *A Phoenix Too Frequent*) who is determined to die at her husband's grave, subsequently accepts the consolations of the guard at the gallows, and eventually permits her husband's body to be hanged in the place of the stolen corpse of a criminal. In Brecht's play, the action was shifted to the late Middle Ages and the locale to Germany. The present song was entitled "Lucifers Abendlied" (Lucifer's Evening Song). Later, the poem was incorporated in *The Rise and Fall of the City of Mahagonny*. Besides Kurt Weill, Rudolph Wagner-Regeny has set it to music.

2. Lines 1 and 2. All other versions of this poem (in *Taschenpostille, Mahagonny,* and *Gedichte I*) have: "Laßt euch nicht betrügen / Daß Leben wenig ist" (Don't let them tell you that life is worth little). The difference between these conflicting versions hinges on the use of one of two symbols: s or ß.

3. In the *Mahagonny* version of the poem, "den Erlösten" (pious people) was replaced by "den Verwesten" (the decayed).

"Es steht nicht mehr bereit" (There's no life after this). Lit.: nothing more significant is awaiting you.

P. 236 *Vom schlechten Gebiß* (On a Bad Set of Teeth).

Münsterer (p. 30) calls this poem one of Brecht's "most personal": his teeth had already decayed badly while he was still in Augsburg.

4. "dessen Bild in ihren Hirnen schwankt" (whose image wavers in their heads). Lit.: they cannot make up their minds about him. The line may be an allusion to Schiller's famous dictum on Wallenstein (in the prologue to *Wallensteins Lager*): "Schwankt sein Charakterbild in der Geschichte" (history has not arrived at a definitive judgment of his character).

P. 238 *Von seiner Sterblichkeit* (On His Mortality).

First published as "Der Virginienraucher" (The Cigar Smoker) in *Das Tagebuch,* Berlin, March, 1923, this poem was omitted from the *Hauspostille* (1927) but included in the *Taschenpostille* (1926) under its present title (On His Mortality). The B.B. of the previous poem is an alcoholic. The B.B. of this poem is a teetotaler. The contrast tells us something of Brecht's method in self-portraiture.

P. 242 *Von den Sündern in del Hölle* (On the Sinners in Hell).

Written, according to Münsterer (p. 80), in 1917 or even earlier. Concerning the names Müllereisert, Neher, and Pfanzelt, see the note on the "Guide." The poem is a close parody of supplicatory prayers for the dead.

6. "Es käm nicht auf ihn an" (They do not count for much). The phrase implies: Pfanzelt had the unfortunate idea that he doesn't really count, that he cannot change the course of history. Avoiding one's responsibility is a frequent theme in Brecht's work. It has central importance, for example, in the plays *Trommeln in der Nacht* (Drums in the Night), 1922, and *Galileo, 1938.*

8, 9. "Hundestein" (dog stone) was a particular spot in Augsburg, near St. Stephen's Church. Brecht would often wait for his friends by the "Hundestein" (cf. Münsterer, p. 110).

9. "in der Höllen" (in Hell) is an obsolete Biblical form of "in der Hölle."

P. 246 *Vom armen B.B.* (On the Poor B.B.).

Written in 1921 (cf. Bertolt Brecht, *Gedichte und Lieder,* Frankfurt, 1962, p. 161).

In this poem, Brecht vaguely imitated the rhythmic patterns of the classical ode as used by German poets of the late eighteenth century. Especially stanzas 7 and 8 are reminiscent of poems by Friedrich Hölderlin (1770–1843).

1. Brecht's parents had moved to Augsburg from Achern in the Black Forest a short time before his birth. The phrase "aus den schwarzen Wäldern" (from the black forests) avoids the geographic designation "Schwarzwald" (Black Forest).

7. "unterhalten" (amuse) can also mean "sustain."

8. Brecht's motif of the disappearance of cities may have been inspired by Rimbaud. Cf. Enid Starkie, *Arthur Rimbaud,* rev. ed., New York, 1947, pp. 303–04.